THE SUN DANCE PEOPLE

THE SUN DANCE PEOPLE

The Plains Indians, their past and present

Written and photographed by **RICHARD ERDOES**

A VINTAGE SUNDIAL BOOK RANDOM HOUSE   NEW YORK

*To my wife Jean, who walked the Indian trail with me
and to Henry Crow Dog, whose picture is on the cover*

Vintage Sundial Books are published by Alfred A. Knopf, Inc., Pantheon
Books, and Random House, Inc.

First Vintage Sundial Edition, October 1972. Originally published by
Alfred A. Knopf, Inc., in May 1972.

Library of Congress Cataloging in Publication Data
Erdoes, Richard. The Sun Dance people.
(A Vintage sundial book, VS-3)   1. Indians of North America—Great
Plains.   I. Title.   [E78.G73E7 1972b]   970.4′8   72-3246
ISBN 0-394-70803-2 (pbk.)

CONTENTS

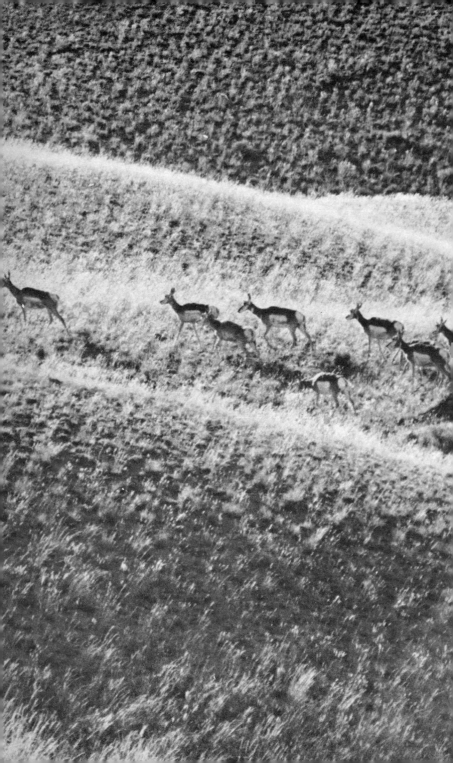

1 ▪ AN OCEAN OF GRASS

*What do we want with this
vast, worthless area,
this region of savages and
wild beasts, of deserts,
of shifting sands, and
whirlwinds of dust,
of cactus and prairie dogs?*

DANIEL WEBSTER

Over a hundred years ago—before the Civil War—maps of the
United States contained a huge, blank area which bore the simple
legend, Indian Territory. It covered an immense region spreading
westward from the Mississippi to the Rocky Mountains and down
from the Canadian border to the arid highlands of Arizona and New
Mexico. There were no towns or settlements within this largely
unknown region—it was the great hunting grounds of the Plains
Indians.

Before the gold-rush days of the 1840's, few white men had ventured inside the Indian Territory. A few surveying parties sent by the
government, a handful of bold travelers driven by a romantic quest
for the unknown, and trappers in search of beaver pelts brought back
their tales to the cities of the East. These were fantastic stories of
endless prairies, innumerable buffalo, and fierce, untamable savages.
Not all travelers returned. Many left their bones on the wind-swept
prairies. The Great Plains was no place for the greenhorn or the
casual visitor.

The surveyors and trappers, who often told conflicting stories,
all agreed on one thing: the West was a wasteland, unfit for white
human habitation, unsuitable for farming or cattle raising. It should,
in the words of Zebulon Pike, "be left to the uncivilized aborigines."

Curiously enough, the same men also agreed on one other thing:

the prairie gave them a feeling of freedom and happiness such as they had never experienced before. It had an enchantment, a mysterious quality, that none of them could explain. It made them forget their families and farms, their soft beds and safe homes in the East. They loved the wilderness with a fierce intensity, and for its sake they endured any hardship and danger. Many of them married Indian women and lived with the wild tribes, losing themselves forever in the vast, uncharted land.

What kind of land was it?

In 1820 Major Stephen Long coined a phrase to describe the Plains. He called it the Great American Desert. This expression was so widely repeated and accepted that it created a certain amount of misunderstanding. As late as 1853 it induced Jefferson Davis, then Secretary of War, to establish a camel corps for use in the West.

While it is true that large parts of the Plains were arid and poor farming country by the standards of the time, only very small areas could be called deserts. The main feature of the Plains was the tree-less prairie, the famous Sea of Grass, the feeding ground of millions of buffaloes. It stretched as far as the eye could see, wave after wave of rolling hills disappearing into purple infinity. Its surface was forever agitated by the rippling winds, and the undulating mass of swaying, rustling grass gave many early travelers the feeling of being surrounded by a special kind of dry ocean.

The eastern plains, with plentiful rainfall, were known as tall-grass country. Today this is the Midwestern Corn Belt with its large, prosperous farms. Across the Missouri the country became drier. Here the grass was shorter, but the soil was still good, with a thick, black layer of fertile sod. This was a country of bluffs, gulches, buttes, and washes.

South of the Niobrara River, in what is now Nebraska and eastern Colorado, the prairie was as flat as a tabletop. The monotony

Early travelers, seeing the wavelike effect of the wind sweeping across the plains, often referred to the prairie as the Sea of Grass.

of the landscape was relieved here and there by spectacular erosions, given such fanciful names as Jail House Rock or Chimney Rock, which served as landmarks for the early pioneers. The prairie was also a land of rivers, many of them famous in Western history: the

Missouri, the Platte, the Powder, the Niobrara, the Tongue, the Snake, the Yellowstone, the Bighorn. Along the riverbanks grew clumps of trees, most numerous among them the cottonwood with its silvery leaves, sacred to many Indian tribes. The Plains made for rough traveling. Indians and whites alike wore leggings of deerskin to protect themselves against the sharp spikes and thorns of an endless variety of prairie plants.

Ever before the eyes of the trapper or hunter were the distant ranges of the Rockies, Captain Meriwether Lewis's "Shining Moun-

The American buffalo provided the Plains Indian with everything he needed for his existence.

Prairie dog "towns" dotted the plains, and the antics of these little animals must have delighted Indians and white travelers alike.

tains." Snowcapped, tantalizing, and beckoning, they rose abruptly out of the Plains. The clear air made them seem much closer than they actually were, as many a westbound traveler discovered to his sorrow. A formidable barrier, they formed the western border of the Plains Indians' domain—the Teton, the Big Horn, the Beartooth, and the Medicine Bow ranges.

Halfway between the Missouri River and the Rockies, in the northwestern corner of South Dakota, rose the Paha-Sapa, the Black Hills, the sacred lands of the Sioux. At night it was thought that its rocks turned into spirits that talked like human beings. Its needle-shaped spires were the home of mighty spirits known as Thunderbirds. The clear stream waters of the Paha-Sapa had magic powers to cure many illnesses.

Not far from the cool and wooded Black Hills spread the "Mauvaises Terres," the Badlands, shunned by whites and Indians alike, a forbidding, waterless landscape of fantastic erosions, sculpted and shaped by wind and weather into likenesses of strange monsters. The floor of the Badlands was strewn with the gigantic bones of long-extinct animals—the mammoth, cave bear, and the woolly rhinoceros. These, the Indians thought, were the bones of evil spirits and thunderhorses of unimaginable size. Side by side with these bones of huge animals, but many millions of years older, lay petrified seashells, ammonites, and the remains of ancient squid, which to the Indians looked like bolts of lightning turned into stone. The mother-of-pearl surface of these fossils was still shiny and iridescent, as if they had just emerged from the waters. They came from a time long before the arrival of the first human beings, when warm oceans covered the Great Plains.

Midway between the Badlands and the Rockies, a gigantic tower of basalt rose abruptly from the prairie to a height of over a thousand feet. Its flanks were streaked with long strips of lava. The Indians said that these were the scratch marks of a giant bear who had tried to claw his way up to the top to capture two maidens who had taken refuge there. Luckily, a young brave shot the bear with a magic arrow and rescued the maidens. Later, to the whites, it was known as Devil's Tower.

Northwest from Devil's Tower was another strange and beautiful country along the Yellowstone, or Elk River, as the Indians called it. Here the earth rumbled and bubbling, multicolored pools spewed forth boiling water. Here were deep canyons and towering waterfalls which dissolved into rainbow-colored spray. South of this strange, steaming land was Jackson Hole, the mountain retreat and place of rendezvous for the fur trappers.

The Great Plains was a huge, natural game preserve. Besides the uncountable multitudes of buffalo, the prairies were dotted with huge herds of deer and antelope. The forest meadows teemed with elk and moose, while the high slopes were the home of bighorn sheep and mountain goats. Prairie dog "towns" were spread all over the Plains. Their thousands of plump, short-tailed "town dwellers" filled the air with their shrill warning cries.

All these grass eaters were stalked by the predators, packs of wolves and coyotes, sharp-fanged mountain lions, and bobcats with grandfatherly side whiskers which belied their fierceness. Bears didn't care what they ate, berries or rabbits, wild roots or squirrels. One could get along with the black or brown bears. But not with the huge, evil-tempered grizzlies, who were so ferocious that only the bravest of men would dare to disturb them. Only a brave who had killed a grizzly had earned the right to wear the necklace made of its huge, fear-inspiring claws. And then there were the smaller fur bearers—foxes, otters, ermines, martens, badgers, and beavers—whose pelts, later, would be exchanged for blankets, powder, knives, or tobacco.

The skies were filled with flocks of innumerable birds, prairie chickens, grouse, and wild turkeys, as well as by hawks and eagles who circled high above the others. The feathers of these creatures could be worn for decoration or, glued to the shaft, could make an arrow fly straight and true.

The Plains was a country of immense sunsets, intense colors, and violent contrasts—a country of scorching heat and bone-chilling cold, of summer hail storms and winter blizzards, of long dry spells and sudden flash floods.

The lives of the people who inhabited the Plains reflected the turbulence of their environment. To the Indians and the mountain men, the Plains was an enormous sports arena in which they could display their skills as hunters, warriors, and horsemen—a place in which to show off one's bravery and endurance. It was a country made for bragging, something which both Indians and mountain men could do very well.

The prairie gave to the people who dwelled in it a sense of personal freedom such as few men have ever enjoyed before or since. To the Indian, moreover, this land was their mother who gave them everything they needed. They were an inseparable part of it, together with the animals, the winds, and the rocks, which were all their brothers.

2 ▪ ON FOOT AND WITHOUT A GUN

*Once we were happy in
our own country and
we were seldom hungry,
for then the two-leggeds
and the four-leggeds lived
together like friends
and there was plenty
for us and for them.*

BLACK ELK SPEAKS

When we think of Indians, we picture in our minds tall, hawked-nosed, keen-eyed men splendidly garbed in streaming war bonnets and decorated, fringed shirts of deerskin. We also imagine them as being heavily armed with gun, shield, lance, and scalping knife, proudly astride their fiery war ponies, impatient to ride on to a fight or tribal hunt.

In reality, however, these Red Knights of the Prairie formed only a small part of America's Indian population. Their golden age—the happy years of riding, raiding, and chasing buffalo—lasted only a few lifetimes.

Throughout history human development has followed a well-established path. Early man in America, as elsewhere was a roaming hunter. He had no permanent home. Every day he covered many miles in search of game to provide his family with food. Some fifteen thousand years ago he stalked and killed animals now long extinct —the mammoth, the woolly rhinoceros, the wild camel. In the ashes of his cooking fires have been found the fossilized bones of these creatures. A beautifully worked, fluted stone arrowhead, a so-called Folsom point, has been found stuck in the bone of an ice-age bison.

The weapons of these early hunters were made of chipped and flaked stone, because the Indians did not know of iron before the white man came. It took the nomads many generations before they learned how to plant and harvest wild corn and squash, becoming part-time farmers in the process. This made a tremendous difference in their lives. Agriculture, even in its most primitive form, meant food when no game could be found. It meant larger numbers of people living in villages, instead of small, scattered hunting parties made up of single families. It meant the beginnings of pottery making. It meant an increase in population, which went together with the increased food supply.

Many tribes had reached this stage of development long before Coronado and his band of Spanish caballeros first entered the Plains in the middle of the sixteenth century. The changeover from hunting to planting, from a nomadic to a settled life, did not come about in a steady, uniform manner. In fact, many tribes rejected farming even in its most primitive form.

Until a very recent date, somewhere between 1700 and 1800, when they acquired horses and guns from the white man, many Plains Indians lived almost exactly as their mammoth-hunting ancestors had lived thousands of years before them. They were very unlike the Plains Indians of our imagination, the proud warriors of Sitting Bull and Crazy Horse. Their life was hard and lacked the splendor and excitement that came with the horse.

In those dim, vanished days, when there was no one to write down their history, the Indians had no domestic animals except the dog. A few tribes ate their dogs, but mostly they were used as beasts of burden. Two poles forming a V-shape were fastened by the point to a dog's shoulder, A bundle, weighing from forty to eighty pounds, was lashed across the poles behind the dogs, the ends of the poles trailing on the ground. This carrying contraption is known to us as a travois, a name given to it by French-Canadian trappers.

A family's worldly goods were contained in the few packs their

These beautifully fluted arrowheads have been found together with the bones of extinct animals. The type shown here is known as Folsom points. They are several thousand years old.

dogs could drag along and whatever the women could carry on their backs. The men did not carry any burdens. They had to remain unencumbered, free to use their arms and weapons at any moment against a game animal or a suddenly emerging enemy.

The fact that the early Plains dwellers had no beast of burden larger than the dog limited their life in a number of ways. They could carry few possessions and thus could not develop a material culture. The stark fight for survival—the daily struggle to feed and clothe themselves—left them little time for arts and crafts. Lacking the means to carry large objects also dictated the kind of dwelling they could have. The roomy, comfortable tepee of later days required, besides a number of buffalo skins, up to twenty long cedar poles for its construction, and neither dogs nor women on foot could have transported them over long distances.

Hunting buffalo was not an easy thing to do if you had to walk.

The animals were constantly on the move and they moved surprisingly fast. Since they could outrun any human being, a herd could disappear overnight. Hunters patiently stalked their prey, crawling on all fours, camouflaged with deerskins and pairs of antlers tied to their heads. Even if, in this way, the men could get near enough to hit a buffalo with their arrows, the wounded animal often got away. A better method to obtain large quantities of meat was to drive a herd over a cliff, a so-called buffalo jump. For this, the cooperation of the whole tribe was needed. The buffaloes were stampeded into a funnel-shaped path lined on both sides with boulders. Rows of men and women, waving skins and branches and making as much noise as possible, hurried the terrified creatures along to their doom.

Many such ancient buffalo jumps can be found today throughout the Plains area. They are easily recognized by the large numbers of bleached bones piled up at the foot of each cliff, which is sometimes covered with simple, scratched-in drawings of animals, spirals, and zigzag lines. These pictographs were a form of hunting magic. They gave the hunters power over the animals—letting them be killed by people who already had "captured" them in the form of a picture.

The farming tribes in semipermanent villages were only a little better off. With one or two crops, an unpredictable climate, and no domesticated animals, they had to make do with the barest necessities. Thus, life on the prairies was harsh and comfortless. The Indians were always hungry, and in the wintertime they often starved.

Within a very short space of time, the world of the tribes was turned upside down, and the wanderers and primitive planters were transformed into the hard-riding Lords of the Plains. Two things brought about this tremendous revolution—the horse and, later, the gun.

The prehistoric Indians have left us many pictographs and petroglyphs. A pictograph (top) is an image *painted on* a cliff; a petroglyph (bottom) is a figure of a man or animal *carved into* a cliff.

Horses were introduced into the New World by the Spaniards during the first half of the sixteenth century. As New Spain grew and expanded to include the area now known as Arizona and New Mexico, horses were brought across the Rio Grande and from then on spread steadily northward. Some horses escaped from their owners and from these grew herds of wild mustangs. It soon became clear that no tribe without horses could long withstand an attack by mounted enemies. Acquisition of the new, strange animal became a matter of sheer survival. Those who could ride raided those who could not. Horseless tribes were often driven out of their home territories.

Experts say that there are six things which make up the true Plains Indian: the horse, the buffalo, the tepee, the warriors' society, the sun dance, and the absence of agriculture. A hard core of tribes were Plains Indians in this pure, extreme sense. They were surrounded by other tribes, who had adopted many features of the Plains culture. Almost all of them had horses and hunted buffalo. Some also had tepees and dressed in the fashion of the Plains, but had no sun dance or warriors' society. Others had both of these things but were settled in villages cultivating their corn and squash fields. Others built their dwellings along rivers and fished.

The outside tribes had arrived by many routes. Along the eastern borders of the Plains, white, English-speaking settlers drove the Indian nations of the Atlantic seaboard before them. For a while this white flood stopped at the Appalachian Mountains. But after the American Revolution it burst through this last barrier, and wave after wave of land-hungry pioneers swarmed into the lands beyond. They did not stop until they reached the Mississippi, which, for a space of time, became the western frontier of the United States.

Nations from the eastern seaboard, the Choctaw, Cherokee, and Delaware, suddenly appeared on the Plains, over a thousand miles away from their ancient homes. At first it was a trickle, then a flood, then a deluge. It ended only when the last of the so-called civilized tribes were forcibly removed, driven from their villages and farms by politicians and land speculators. They were prodded by bayonets along the "Trail of Tears," through the snows of a bitter winter to a new "home" which most of them never reached.

A similar process occurred in the North, in the forests of the Great Lakes region. In this case, though, the Ojibwa, who had acquired guns and steel knives from French traders, used these terrible new weapons to drive the Cheyenne and Sioux from their hunting grounds and corn patches in Minnesota and Wisconsin. Almost overnight, so it seemed, these uprooted corn planters turned into fierce, nomadic horsemen.

All of these displaced tribes were like so many ripples of a gigantic storm that swept the prairies. The result of the population shift was a great mix-up of cultures and languages. A tribe might be surrounded by neighbors belonging to a different language group, while relatives whom they could understand were a thousand miles away. Sedentary tribes found themselves next to the hunting grounds of nomadic peoples. Some had come as refugees, others as conquerors. A few tribes grew powerful while others, weakened by warfare and disease, vanished from the scene. Together, these different nations acted out the great drama of the Plains—a superspectacular unique in human history.

It took the white settlers more than half a century to fill up the land between the Appalachians and the Mississippi. Before the 1840s only a few hundred mountain men, trappers, traders, and soldiers ventured into the Great Plains beyond the river.

As the white nation paused in its westward march, the tribes on the prairie had a chance to parcel out their respective hunting grounds and to maintain a certain balance of power among them-

The area of the Plains culture and those of its neighbors.

selves. Hostile tribes still attacked each other, but Indian warfare was mostly a matter of raids by small bands of warriors. The peoples of the Plains had a great reluctance to challenge their neighbors to a do-or-die battle which could only end in the destruction of one or the other tribe. Such clashes were extremely rare and occurred only as a result of extraordinary circumstances, usually beyond the control of the tribes involved.

Travelers in the early 1800s, such as the members of the Lewis and Clark expedition, or the artists George Catlin and Karl Bodmer who had come to study and paint the Indians, found the tribes distributed in the following way. On the eastern prairies lived many tribes, the Hidatsa (the Willow People) and Mandan in the present North Dakota, the Arikara just below them. The Iowa, Ponca, Oto, Kansa, Osage and Wichita tribes were strung out in a north-south line all the way from Iowa and Nebraska down to Oklahoma and the Texas border. The Santee Sioux were still in Minnesota separated by the Missouri from their brothers, the Teton Sioux, whose tepees were pitched from the west bank of the river to the Black Hills.

Northwest from the Hidatsa lived the Assiniboin, occupying lands in Saskatchewan and North Dakota. Good traders, the Assiniboin were engaged in a never-ending war with their cousins, the Sioux. Farther west, along the Missouri River in Montana, the traveler first came across the Atsina, or Gros Ventre, before meeting the "terrible" Blackfeet, who suffered no white trapper within their boundaries. These formed a confederation with the Blood and Piegan Indians. Also in Montana lived the Flatheads, who got their name because they flattened the heads of their babies to "make them more beautiful."

Below the Atsina, straddling the Montana-Wyoming border, roamed the Crow, also called Absaroke, or Bird People. They were an offshoot of the Hidatsa, friendly to the whites but enemies to all Sioux.

The northernmost Plains tribes were the Sarsi and their eastern neighbors the Cree. The Cree were originally a canoe and snowshoe people, but they had early obtained a great number of trade guns, which they had used with deadly effect to make a home for themselves on the prairie.

Beyond the Rocky Mountains in Idaho dwelled the brave and friendly Nez Percé who bred the famous Appaloosa horses.

Over the central plains, from Wyoming into Colorado, galloped the Cheyenne and their friends and allies the Arapaho. Their western neighbors were the Shoshone, or Snakes. Sacajawea, the young woman who acted as guide and interpreter to Lewis and Clark, belonged to this tribe. Their relatives the warlike Ute lived to the west in Colorado and Utah.

The southernmost Plains Indians were the Kiowa and Comanche. They lived in Oklahoma and Texas but were most of the time on the move, appearing on their swift horses in the most unexpected places. The Comanche, who had moved down from the northern plains, belonged to the Shoshonean family. They were superb horsemen, and American officers called them the "best light cavalry in the world."

This, then, was the kaleidoscopic world of the many tribes which dwelled in the Plains. It was a colorful, short-lived world of splendor and high adventure which lasted until the 1860s and 1870s. Then the Indians were driven into the outdoor prisons which the white man called reservations.

3 ▪ THE SPIRIT DOG

Without the horse the Indian
was a half-starved skulker
in the timber, creeping up
on foot towards the unweary deer.
With the horse he was transformed
into the daring buffalo hunter,
able to procure in a single day
enough food to supply his family
for a year, leaving him free
to sweep the plains with his war
parties along a range of a thousand
miles.

JAMES MOONEY

The Indian is in the saddle from
boyhood to old age, and his favorite
horse is his constant companion . . .
he prizes him more highly than
anything else in his possession.

RANDOLPH B. MARCY

Once, over a million years ago, prehistoric horses roamed the western plains, but for some reason, they died out and vanished from the Western Hemisphere. We do not know how or why. It all happened long before the first human beings came to America, and so the Indians had never seen a horse before the Spaniards brought them to the New World.

When the Plains dwellers first encountered these strange and wonderful beasts which would transform their lives, they had no word to describe them. They could see that these new animals could carry burdens, just like their travois dogs, and so they called the horse Spirit Dog, Holy Dog, Big Dog, Elk Dog, or Medicine Dog.

When Cortés and his band of adventurers set out to conquer the Aztec empire, their steeds terrified the Mexican Indians. At first they thought that horse and rider were one, a strange, supernatural monster, half man and half beast. One of Cortés's cavaliers describes how exultant the Tlascalas were when they managed to kill a horse and discovered that it was mortal, and that the Spaniards, those fearful, white, bearded gods, were after all just men like themselves.

The Spaniards knew that they owed their victories to the fact that they were mounted. They made laws that forbade Indians to own a horse or to be taught how to ride. It was one of those laws which looks fine on paper but is impossible to enforce in real life. In their vast new empire the handful of Spaniards needed Indian servants to do the work. The servants could naturally do their errands faster and better on horseback than on foot. Later, as the Spaniards imported cattle and other livestock, the hacienda owners needed mounted vaqueros, or cowboys, to take care of their herds. These men also had to be Indians. In this way the tribes in New Spain, including the province of New Mexico, became familiar with horses.

It is thought that horses appeared on the southern plains for the first time about 1540. Beginning in that year, Coronado led an expedition of three hundred Spaniards and several thousand Mexican Indians into the unknown regions beyond the Rio Grande. The Spaniards had come in their usual quest for gold and treasure, having heard fantastic tales of the fabled cities of Cibola, where the streets were paved with silver, and gold was cheap and plentiful as iron. Coronado did not lose heart when the cities of Cibola turned out to be poor, wretched pueblos whose shining silver was nothing more than the reflection of the midday sun on smooth adobe walls.

The gold, so he was told, was farther north in the land of Quivira, whose ruler had so much of the precious metal that hundreds of

The Indians had no wheel to transport their goods. They used a framework of two poles which were attached to the back of a dog or horse.
We therefore speak of dog and horse travois. It is a French word introduced by Canadian trappers. The travois was much more suited to the
roadless prairie than the wheel.

wagons could not carry it away. That monarch was said to amuse
himself by fastening thousands of golden bells to the branches of the
trees in his shaded park, like so many apples in a Spanish orchard, as
Coronado told his soldiers. Even in a light breeze, the tinkling of
the bells made a most wonderful music. The Spanish looked for
Quivira in what is now Kansas. They did not find it, but they found
Indians with large dogs who carried their masters' belongings on
travois poles.

For the first time the Spaniards also saw immense herds of huge, humped, shaggy beasts which they called Indian cattle. They had come, however, to look for gold and not for buffalo or dog travois. Furious and disappointed, they killed their Indian guide, a man called the Turk because he wore a headband which looked like a Mohammedan turban, and started on their thousand-mile ride back to Mexico.

Unfortunately, nobody has left us an account of what the Plains Indians thought of their first encounter with the white man and his horse. There are many charming legends of how some horses of Coronado's expedition escaped and eventually grew into the vast herds of wild horses that roamed the prairies. These herds, so the story went, were sired by the great white stallion, a superhorse of pure Arabian stock. It is always sad to question a beautiful legend, but Coronado had only two mares, and the Spaniards were not likely to carelessly lose these precious animals. Even if a single horse got away, the chances of its surviving and starting a herd were very small indeed. A more likely explanation is that the wild herds came about as a result of the great Pueblo Revolt of 1680.

During this uprising many of the Spaniards of New Mexico were killed. The survivors, who fled to El Paso, had to leave their herds of horses behind, which either went wild or fell into the hands of the Indians. By 1700 many tribes owned horses, though some of them had to wait almost a hundred years longer. While the Indians living closest to New Mexico were, as a rule, the first to acquire the animals, the spread of the horse did not automatically proceed along a straight south-to-north path. Sometimes there was a kind of leap-frogging by which a tribe would learn to ride earlier than its southern neighbors. But usually the northern nations were the last ones to get hold of a Spirit Dog.

With the horses, a new, golden age began for the Plains Indian. The hunting of buffalo became an exhilarating sport, rather than an

Horse racing and betting were things the Indians did not have to learn from the white man. They were their favorite sports from the moment they acquired the horse in the eighteenth century . . .

. . . and they still are . . .

exhausting search for food. It was now easy to follow the herds, and there was always plenty of meat to eat. Space, once a restraining prison, became a playing field.

Adapting the travois to the horse brought about a new ease of transport. The poles of the travois were supple and yielding. On the roadless prairie they gave a smoother ride than the ox-drawn wagons of the white settlers. On a travois a horse could drag a load four or five times heavier than it could have carried on its back. The horse travois also meant the end of pitiful, small shelters. Tribe after tribe adopted the tepee, the large, conical tent with lodgepoles that were up to thirty feet high.

This new ease of transport also resulted in a new wealth of possessions which could now be carried along, and the tribes developed a new material culture. With hunting so much easier and faster, the people had more time to spend decorating their weapons, their clothing, and their dwellings. The Plains Indians turned into dandies.

The horse also made it possible to get many buffalo and other skins to swap with the traders for blankets and beads, knives and hatchets, kettles, or vermilion color to paint one's face. One could even get a gun. No wonder that the horse became an Indian's prize possession. A man's favorite war or buffalo horse was always tethered near his tepee and was as much adorned as his master.

Horses became the favorite currency of the Plains. In some tribes a gift of two or more horses was given to a girl's family by the intended husband. Ownership of many horses was a symbol of a man's skill and bravery, as he had to acquire them by raiding the enemy. If a warrior died, his favorite war pony was killed to serve him on his ride to the spirit world. This was very much like a Viking funeral, where a dead chieftain was burned together with his longship.

The nomads of the Plains became wonderfully skilled horsemen. A new race of centaurs developed, as horse and rider seemed to grow into one living being. A Plains Indian afoot became unnatural. The artist George Catlin wrote: "A Comanche on his feet is out of his element . . . but the moment he lays his hand upon his horse, he gracefully flies away like a different being."

Indian boys could ride almost before they learned to walk. One of the feats of Indian horsemanship, often commented upon by whites, was the ability to hook one leg over a pony's back and lie flat against its flank while riding at full speed. Then, using the horse as a living shield between themselves and their enemies, the Indians would shoot arrows from underneath its neck or belly.

The Plains people were not only superb riders but also excellent breeders of horses. The Cayuse tribe was so good at it that the word Cayuse became the universal name for the Western pony. The Nez Percé bred the famous Appaloosas, prized above all others.

In time the Indian pony became a distinct type of horse, sturdy, fast, and long-winded. Unlike their Spanish ancestors, most Indian horses were pintos, with brown or black splotches on a light coat.

One way to capture wild horses, especially fast stallions, was to surround them with teams of hunters who would take their turns stalking and pursuing a wild herd. As a hunter or his horse grew tired, he was quickly replaced by others. The wild mustangs were not permitted to rest, graze, or drink. At the end of three or four days they were so exhausted that a rider could get near enough to lasso one.

What happened next was described by Catlin: "Once he has thrown a noose around its neck the Indian instantly dismounts, letting the lasso pass out gradually through his hands, by which their speed is checked and they are 'choked-down' until the wild horse falls for want of breath and lies helpless on the ground—then the Indian advances closely towards the horse's head, until he fastens

There are not enough horses on the Cheyenne reservation in Montana for all the boys who want to ride. But Indians are used to sharing their possessions and pleasures. The hundred-year-old print above shows that some things have not changed.

a pair of hobbles on the animal's forefeet. Then the lasso is loosened giving the horse a chance to breathe. He puts a noose around its underjaw, by which he gets great power over the affrightened animal, which begins rearing and plunging. As he advances . . . the horse makes every possible effort to get away, until its power is exhausted and it becomes covered with foam, and at last yields to the powers of man. He gradually places his hand on the animal's nose and over its eyes and at length breathes into its nostrils. It soon becomes docile and he can lead or ride it into camp. Great care is taken not to subdue the spirit of the animal."

Before a fight the Sioux and Cheyenne always raced their ponies back and forth to give them their second wind. During the Indian wars, the heavy, grain-fed horses of the U.S. Cavalry were no match for the fleet-footed, strong-hearted Spirit Dogs of the Plains.

From the point of view of the anthropologist, the transformation of one-time corn planters, no matter how primitive, into nomadic hunters on horseback is a step backwards along the path of human development. This path is supposed to lead "upwards" from hunter, to herdsman, to farmer, to tool maker (technocrat). We can be sure, however, that the Plains Indian did not see it this way as he joyfully raced his horse over his beloved prairie, fragrant with the scent of sage and sweet grass.

The horse is no longer a necessity for the Indians living on today's reservations, but the love for the animal still lingers on. There is no lack of powwows, tribal rodeos, and horse races where one can show one's skill as a rider. But there are not as many horses as in the old days. It is a common sight to see two, or even three, young Indian boys or girls on one horse, smiling happily. One horse for two riders is better than no horse at all.

4 ▪ "INDIAN CATTLE"

Without the horse, life on the Plains would have been hard and shorn of its glory. Without the buffalo it would have come to an end. The buffalo, or North American bison, covered the prairies in incredible numbers—fifty million or more in the estimate of some early travelers. Nobody will ever know for sure.

Seen from a distant mountaintop, some areas of the prairie at times looked like one huge, dark, squirming mass, a moving carpet of buffalo. Mountain men told of making their way through herds stretching for a hundred miles. To those fortunate enough to view it, the sight of the prairie covered from horizon to horizon with the large, majestic beasts remained unforgettable.

The buffalo gave to the Indian his shelter, his fuel, his clothing, and most of the utensils he needed for his daily life. No part of the animal was wasted. The list of articles made from the various parts of the buffalo was almost inexhaustible.

Buffalo meat formed the main part of the Indian's diet. Even the contents of the animal's stomach and the intestines slightly roasted over a fire were eaten. Full of vegetable matter, they were a source of much-needed vitamins. Meat which was not consumed at once was dried and smoked. This "buffalo jerky" was stored up for the long and lean winter months. Meat, fat, and marrow pounded into a paste and mixed with berries was called pemmican. It was a highly nutritious, concentrated energy food. A handful of pemmican could keep a man going for a whole day.

At the end of the nineteenth century, the buffalo was almost extinct. It was saved by the wisdom and concern of a small handful of men. Now the herds are growing again in most of our western national parks.

The hide had many uses. Sixteen to twenty skins sewn together made a large tepee. Heavily furred winter skins were used as robes, beds, and blankets. A small piece could be made into a warm cap. Tanned hides were fashioned into moccasins and leggings. They were sewn together or singly stretched over a frame of bent willow sticks to make "bull boats" for river crossings.

The thick skin from the neck, dried and hardened, became a warrior's shield. A good one would turn an arrow. Some even withstood the impact of a musket ball, but not the bullet from a high-powered rifle. A patch of rawhide stretched over a hoop made a fine resonant drum. Lassos and bridles were made from rawhide thongs. When wet, the thongs were used to lash the stone head of a war club to its shaft. As the rawhide dried, it tightened firmly around the stone. Parfleches were giant envelopes of scraped, parchmentlike skin. Painted with colorful designs, parfleches were used like luggage to carry one's possessions. Soft saddlebags, decorated with quill and beadwork, served a similar purpose. The sinews of the buffalo were used by the women as thread for sewing.

The stomach was a natural cooking pot, the bladder a water bag. The horns were made into a headdress for a medicine man or carved into spoons and cups. The skull, painted with red dots, became the central part of the sun dance altar. This was only natural, as the all-important, life-giving buffalo was a sacred animal.

The ribs were tied together to make sleds for the children, and shoulder blades became hoes. The leg bones were made into fleshers, scrapers, knives, and awls. Small, delicate bones were made into sewing needles. A paste made from the brains was used as a tanning acid for the hides. Hooves were boiled down into glue. The dried dung, so-called buffalo chips, was the main fuel on the treeless plains. Even the tail had its use. It made a fine fly swatter.

A tribal buffalo hunt was an important event. It was almost like going to war. For a young lad it was a fine opportunity to show off his skill and courage. It was a solemn undertaking, well planned and well policed.

Sometimes a hunt was preceded by a buffalo dance or other religious ceremony to obtain the help of the supernatural powers. The whole camp would buzz with excitement when the scouts brought news that a big herd had been sighted. Soon the crier, or herald, would ride around the circle of tepees, dressed in all his finery. The crier, a respected older man, would shout in a loud, melodious voice:

> *"Many Buffalo, I hear,*
> *Many Buffalo, I hear,*
> *They are coming now,*
> *They are coming now,*
> *Sharpen your arrows,*
> *Sharpen your knives!"*

In a flurry of frenzied activity, the women would dismantle the tepees, stuff their household belongings into parfleches, and fasten their bundles on travois poles.

Young men acting as the camp police, the akicita, would gallop back and forth, assigning everybody his proper place in the marching order. It was their responsibility to see to it that no eager hunter would selfishly ride ahead, spooking or stampeding the buffalo and thereby endangering the success of the whole enterprise. With their unstrung bows and whips, the camp police beat anyone who disobeyed their orders, even if he was a chief. Serious offenses against hunting discipline could be punished by burning the guilty man's tepee, or even killing his favorite horse.

Mothers were warned to watch their children, especially their high-spirited boys, and to keep them out of mischief. Order quickly came out of confusion, as everyone was eager to start out. Far ahead ranged the scouts, keeping an eye on the buffalo.

A few miles behind them came the main column, its flanks protected by warriors. First came the four pipe bearers, or advisers, or shirt wearers, or sacred buffalo-stick holders, depending on the tribe. They were very important persons and well aware of this fact. To their care were entrusted the magic medicine objects, upon which depended the happy outcome of the hunt. They were dressed in their finest feathered, fringed, and beaded costumes. Anyone who dared

The buffalo, who gave his flesh so that the people might live, was sacred to all Plains tribes. He was honored by prayers and ceremonies, such as the dance shown.

to cross their path was immediately knocked from his horse by the camp police.

Behind the pipe bearers rode the chiefs in all their splendor. And then, helter-skelter, came the fantastic jumble of women and children, a joyous multitude of young and old. On top of each horse travois perched one or two women and several children. Astride their high-pommeled, beautifully beaded women's saddles sat the young mothers, vainly trying to whip their old horses into a faster gait. Plodding steadily along, eyes half-closed, ears nodding, the old horses paid not the slightest attention to the tuggings and kickings.

Sometimes a baby's cradleboard was slung over the end of a lodgepole, which would bob madly up and down. Now and then a fast-stepping horse would spill its squealing load of youngsters, to the great delight of the other travelers. Little girls had their arms full of yelping puppies which were their special playthings. Loose horses cantered back and forth, their shrill neighing mingled with the barking of a multitude of dogs.

Boys scampered about excitedly, shooting arrows, playing the hoop game, or beating the bushes for rabbits and other small game. As the happy cavalcade rushed along, it gave a fine impression of the days of the free and easy prairie life.

As soon as the Indians reached the herd, the hunt began in earnest. The Plains people were forever mindful of the poor, and especially those who could no longer care for themselves. Nobody was allowed to go without food or shelter. Often the crier would admonish the members of a warrior society: "Young men, you hunt well, we know. You never fail. Today you will feed the helpless. Old people who have no sons. Little ones who have no fathers. Women whose husbands are dead. What you kill today will be for them!"

The young hunters rode their specially trained buffalo ponies which, guided only by the pressure of their riders' knees, would anticipate every move of an enraged buffalo. A hunter rode up to the buffalo from the rear. Nobody in his right mind would approach them from the front where a stampeding herd could crush and trample him to death. It took courage and know-how to be a good hunter.

Lieutenant Frederic Ruxton, who traveled on the prairies in the 1840s, said: "No animal requires so much killing as the buffalo. Unless shot through the lungs or spine, they usually escape."

But with the Indians, the killing was done with bow and arrow, even if the hunter owned a gun. Powder and lead were costly and hard to come by. One could also shoot arrows faster than one could reload the old trade muskets with their cumbersome ramrods.

Each hunter had arrows of his own design and color pattern, so

Hunting the buffalo took skill and courage. The killing of his first buffalo was one of the proudest moments in the life of every young Indian.

that it was easy to tell which animals he had killed. A man who needed more than four arrows to bring down his quarry was considered a poor shot. A horseman's bow had necessarily to be short, but it could be very powerful. Eyewitnesses saw a Cheyenne warrior kill two buffaloes with one shot, the arrow passing through both animals.

A good buffalo horse swerved and turned as soon as it heard the twang of the bowstring. It knew how to keep out of the range of the horns of the buffalo, who was dangerous after being hit. Killed animals were quickly butchered. The liver was usually eaten raw on the spot. Soon travois heaped with meat arrived at the nearby established campsite, and in no time the women were busily preparing

The Indian's church is the sky and the earth; his altar a buffalo and a pipe.

the meat or stretching the hides on wooden frames for scraping and tanning. This was a time for dancing and singing, and most of all for good eating.

"Buffalo meat is indescribably tender, fiberless, and gamey," wrote an enthusiastic traveler, "the greatest meat man has ever fed on."

The meat was broiled on skewers or boiled in the animal's stomach pouch, or in a skin bag full of water into which red-hot stones were dropped. In the absence of salt and pepper, gall and a little gunpowder were sometimes used for seasoning. Tongues were the greatest delicacies. They were usually reserved for the warriors, though an enterprising boy would sometimes succeed in snatching one up, gleefully making off with it at high speed to the amusement of the whole camp.

The lean, meat-hungry hunters could really eat. Eight pounds of meat was the normal, daily ration for an active man. At last the feasters would lie exhausted from so much riding, hunting, dancing, and eating. The camp would grow still, and even the dogs would sleep. Out on the dark prairie, a circle of glowing dots might move a little closer—the light of the campfires being reflected in the eyes of the many coyotes attracted by the wonderful smell of roasted meat.

5 ▪ LIFE IN A TEPEE

*A beautiful tepee
is like a good mother.
She hugs her children
to her and protects them
from heat and cold,
dust storms or rain.*

INDIAN PROVERB

An early nineteenth century visitor to the Plains was likely to come across the earth lodges of the sedentary tribes before he saw any tepees. This was especially true if he traveled by boat along the Missouri or Platte rivers. These would be the Hidatsa, Mandan, or Pawnee tribes, living in permanent villages, often fortified and fenced in as a protection against marauding enemies.

George Catlin has left us a wonderful description of the two Mandan villages he visited between 1830 and 1836:

"I have this morning perched myself upon the top of one of the earth-covered lodges, having the whole village beneath and about me, with its warriors, dogs, and horses in motion; its scalp-poles waving over my head; its green prairies in full view; with the din and bustle of the thrilling panorama that is about me. . . . On the tops of the lodges are to be seen groups standing and reclining whose picturesque appearances it would be hard to describe. Beyond these, groups are engaged in games; some are also to be seen manufacturing robes and dresses; and others fatigued with amusements, have stretched their limbs to enjoy the luxury of sleep while basking in the sun. . . . On the roofs of the lodges are also buffalo skulls, skin canoes, sleds, and other things. And suspended on poles are displayed the scalps of warriors . . . exposed as evidence of warlike deeds. On other poles are the warriors' shields, quivers, and medicine bags; and here and there a sacrifice of red cloth, offered up to the Great Spirit."

The Mandan lodges, from the roof of which Catlin enjoyed his splendid view, were permanent dwellings of a settled people, who had otherwise adopted the customs and way of life of their more nomadic neighbors. The Mandan lodges were shaped like beehives, made of logs and covered with sod packed around the outside. It is possible that in many ways they served as models for the sod houses of the early white settlers, which were built on a similar principle but had a rectangular shape.

The earthen floors of the lodges were clean, well-swept, and hardened to a polished glaze. The roof rested on four large poles and had an opening at its top to let the smoke from the cooking fires escape. The dwellings were very large and roomy, with a diameter of from forty to sixty feet. In the center was the fireplace. Around the inside of the wall ran an earthen bench. Besides being filled with a profusion of household goods, weapons, and religious paraphernalia, the lodges had ample room for the owner's family, as well as his horse and dogs.

The Mandan lodges were sturdy structures, a safe refuge, too, during a tornado. The lodges' tunnellike entrances always faced east. It was the same with the tepees of the other tribes. Pointing the entrance east was a turning toward the rising sun and had a religious meaning. But it had also a practical side: rain and snow came mostly from the west.

The Caddo and Wichita of the southern plains built thatched grass huts that reminded early explorers of the tropical dwellings of Africans or South Sea Islanders. Overlapping layers of grass kept these lodges cool and waterproof.

Of all the dwellings of the Plains, the tepee was the most widespread. It was wonderfully adapted for the roving life of the prairie and suited the Indians so well that some of the semisedentary tribes, such as the Hidatsa, gave up their earth lodges to become tent dwellers.

Mandan lodges were made of logs and covered with sod packed around the outside. They were warm in the winter and cool during the hot summer months.

Though tepees varied in size from tribe to tribe—the Crow were reputed to have the largest ones, with the longest lodgepoles—the basic construction and appearance was everywhere the same. Simply speaking, the tepee was a cone made up of ten to twenty poles and a number of buffalo hides sewn together. Sixteen skins made a nice, roomy, family tepee.

Indians are a deeply spiritual people, and even commonplace things had for them a religious meaning. It was only natural for the tepee to have a symbolism of its own. The floor of the tepee represented the earth on which we live, the walls the sky, and the poles the yearning upward to the "ones above." The tepee's roundness was

The sod house of the early white settler was in many ways similar to a Mandan earth-lodge. Both were made of the same materials, but the settler's house was square while the Indian's lodge was round.

a reminder of the sacred life circle which has no beginning and no end. Behind a tepee's fire pit was an earth altar, where incense of wacanga, aromatic sweet grass, was burned. The owner's pipe and medicine bundles were kept there. A family's lodge was a circle within the larger camp circle. In this ring of tepees, every lodge had its specially appointed place. In the center of the camp stood the medicine lodge, larger than all the others. It contained the tribe's most sacred possessions upon which the well-being of the people depended. Among the Sioux, the most important was the sacred peace pipe. Among the Northern and Southern Cheyenne, it was the holy buffalo hat and the sacred arrow bundles.

This is the tepee of Two Moons, a famous Cheyenne chief who fought General Custer. This photograph, taken in the 1890s, tells much about Indian life. The women do most of the work. They put up the tepee, cook, and hang up the jerked meat on drying racks.

Just as the entrance of each single tepee faced east, so the whole camp circle was left open in the direction of the sunrise.

The camp of one band could again be part of a still larger circle or circles—the gathering of all the tribes of a nation. The sacred seven campfires of the Sioux were encompassed by the endless horizon of sky and plain. The tepee, camp circle, earth, sky, sun, and universe thus formed a harmonious entity.

A tepee was often decorated with a red stripe representing the earth, or some other abstract religious symbol. Sometimes it was beautifully painted with scenes from its owner's life—the enemies he had conquered, the wounds he had received, or the many horses he had captured.

One characteristic of the Plains tepee was its "ears"—two smoke flaps which could be moved by two poles to direct the flow of the wind, thereby preventing smoke and smarting eyes inside. The tepee's inside was cozy and inviting. The flickering fire in the center gave warmth and light. An inner curtain of scraped hides, painted with geometrical designs, kept out the draft. Even during the heat of summer, the wind-cooled tepee was a comfortable place. Decorated parfleches and backrests made of willow sticks were standard equipment and very pleasing to the eye.

Indians are often wrongly depicted as a scowling, stolid, unsmiling race. This was the face they often showed the white men who cheated, mistreated, and looked down upon them. In reality there were few people more disposed to laughter and good companionship than the Plains Indians. They loved a feast, a happy talk, a friendly smoke. Consequently there was much coming and going between the tepees and lodges.

Life in and around the tepee was regulated by traditional rules of good behavior. In many tribes an open entrance flap meant "Walk right in, everybody." A closed flap implied "Better call out, announce yourself, and wait until you are invited." Two crossed sticks over the entrance were equivalent to saying "We are out" or "We don't want any guests right now." A deer-hoof rattle often served as a door bell.

Visitors coming for dinner politely brought their own pots and eating gear. Upon entering a tepee, men turned to the right and sat down in their proper places. Women moved to the left, the ladies' quarters. It was not polite to step over a man's legs or to come between him and the fire. The right thing was to pass around and behind him. Men sat cross-legged, women with their legs tucked in at their side. The host was seated in his place of honor in the rear of the lodge. He opened each gathering with a prayer and set a little morsel of food aside for the spirits of the departed.

He urged his guests to eat heartily and to take home what was left. He was always the last to help himself. Men were served first, women and children later.

Men talked one at a time and did not expect to be interrupted. Good storytellers were always welcome. A special prayer was sometimes said to help a man tell a particular story straight, without forgetting any important details. Occasionally, storytelling contests took place between members of two warrior societies. An umpire holding a bundle of sticks in his hands would call out questions such as, "Who has rescued a wounded friend during a fight?" Some man on either team might answer, "I have done it." He would then tell the story of his exploit and name his witnesses. If the umpire was satisfied, he would give the man a stick to put into the ground before him. The team winding up with the most sticks would be declared the winner.

Inevitably, there would be the ceremonious smoking of the pipe. This, too, was a form of prayer. Men would not accept the pipe unless it was passed to them in the right way, clockwise, with the stem pointing toward the left.

A story is told of a U.S. general who smoked the peace pipe with the Sioux. When it was his turn to smoke, he carefully wiped the mouthpiece with his handkerchief. The Indian who received the pipe next, looked long and hard at the general and then took out his knife and cut the mouthpiece off.

A big camp-circle of tepees was a beautiful sight. These Crow tepees are no longer made of buffalo skins, but of canvas. Buffalo hides were already hard to obtain sixty years ago, when this picture was taken.

In the old days Indians used to say that white men did not know how to behave or to be polite. Later on they learned to accept this fact—white men just had to be forgiven for being so badly brought up.

At night, with the sparks flying from the smoke holes, and the light shining faintly through the tepee walls, the camp circle was a beautiful sight. After the last smoke, the host solemnly cleaned the pipe. This was the signal that the feast was over, and everybody got up and went home.

Indians today still like to get together and tell a good story. They continue the tradition of speechmaking raised to a fine art. They still like to pass the pipe around. "A good talk," so they say, "is better than watching T.V."

At a tribal fair, rodeo, or sun dance, a visitor can still see a handful of fine, decorated tepees, but the Indians of today have to

At the annual Crow Fair in Montana many families put up their tepees— as many as a hundred or more.

live in houses—white-man style. The older homes are often log cabins similar to those which the early settlers and miners put up. They are simple and sturdy, often without electricity or tap water. They have an old-fashioned coziness, but no modern conveniences. As many Indians are very poor, their homes are sometimes rural slums of tarpaper shacks and rusty house trailers. These are unhealthy and do not protect the people who dwell in them against the summer heat or the bitter cold of a prairie winter. Lately, the government has started many housing projects of neat-looking, inexpensive, modern, bungalow-type homes. But if an Indian does not keep up his monthly payments, such a home could be dragged away by a truck and given to somebody else.

Being inside a modern reservation home is still often very much the same as sitting inside a tepee, as the same rules of behavior are being observed. "But," the Indians also say, "there's no magic in a tarpaper shack or a rusty house trailer. No, not even in a modern prefab house built by the government. There's no power in a square house, it doesn't stand for something like a tepee does. It's just a place to sleep."

"But it's not the house which is so important," added an old Indian lady. "If you have a tepee soul, a tepee spirit, you can do all right even in a square, white man's house."

This painting of Big Elk, an Omaha Indian living near the Missouri River, shows the famous warrior of the Plains as he appeared to the artist George Catlin in 1883.

6 ▪ THE DANGEROUS GAME

I am a fox,
I am supposed to die.
If there is anything difficult,
If there is anything dangerous,
That is for me to do!

SONG OF THE TOKALA, THE
KIT FOX WARRIOR SOCIETY

For the Plains Indian, the game of war was a glorious sport, and it played a very important role in his life. He did not make war as the white man did. His aim was not to kill or to conquer. The leader of a war party was disgraced if he lost so much as a single man, even if his raid was a success. Rather than risk the life of one of his own band, the leader would often let an enemy get away.

Indian warriors rarely fought big battles in which the whole tribe took part. Their warfare was rather like a medieval tournament, fought according to certain well-established rules.

The motive for going to war was a young man's desire for personal glory. In no other way could he gain a reputation, be a respected member of a warrior's society, or rise to chieftainship. In no other way could he gain the admiration of the young women of his tribe. A man gained war honors, similar to a white soldier earning his medals, by "counting coup." *Coup* is a French word meaning "blow," and it is widely used to describe certain brave deeds of a Plains warrior.

Killing a man did not necessarily count as a coup. A coward with a gun or bow could do this without much danger to himself. Even the taking of a scalp was not too important. But riding up to an enemy to touch him with your lance, or coup stick, while he was alive and armed was definitely a first class coup.

Touching with the hand was an even greater deed. Among the Blackfoot Indians, taking away the gun of a living enemy was the biggest coup. Receiving a wound, especially in front, rated high, but rescuing a friend, unhorsed and surrounded by enemies, ranked even higher.

Shooting from an ambush was a thing of no account. Riding back and forth in front of your enemies, exposing yourself to their fire, brought admiring yells from friend and foe alike. Killing a man with a knife was more honorable than bringing him down with a long lance.

The rules for playing at war were sometimes strange and complicated. A warrior might kill an enemy at great danger to himself, but someone else might dash up to count the first coup on the victim's body and gain all the glory. The second man to touch a fallen foe counted the second coup. Among some tribes, as many as four or five coups could be counted. These were, of course, much less valuable than the first.

Oddly enough, coups were also counted on women and even children. One could even count coup upon a thing. For instance, the scouts who were sent out to find a cottonwood, which would serve as a sun dance pole, rode up to the tree as if it were an enemy and counted coup upon it. But this was a symbolic deed. It brought respect, but no war honors.

Deeds of mercy aroused admiration. Sitting Bull, the great Sioux chief and medicine man, in his youth spared the life of a brave Assiniboin lad, who boldly faced a whole band of Sioux warriors. Sitting Bull adopted him as his own brother and thereby gained great honor. This boy grew up to become a famous warrior and re-

Warriors sometimes depicted their brave deeds on buffalo skins or on the sides of their tepees.

paid his debt to Sitting Bull by dying in defense of the man who had saved his life.

War was also a path to wealth, which was counted in the number of horses a man owned. Horse stealing was an integral part of Plains warfare. As a matter of fact, a great majority of all warlike enterprises were raids on the enemies' horse herds. A man could make a great reputation by being a pony thief. War honors were determined by the amount of difficulty encountered. Running off the enemy's herd was a great deed. But the high point of a young warrior's life was to steal a chief's favorite war horse right from beside his owner's tepee in the middle of a hostile camp circle. This feat was rated equal to a first coup.

Nor was a young man arriving home from a raid bashful in letting everyone know of the great deeds he had done. Often he would recount them and act them out before an admiring audience. In addition, there was visual evidence of his bravery. The feathers in his hair were notched, cut, and painted to tell of the wearer's exploits. A feather with a red dot meant a wound received. Other feathers, trimmed in various ways, would stand for a first or second coup.

An established warrior would also proudly paint scenes from his fighting career on the outside of his tepee, his buffalo robe, or his war shirt. A man never lied about the things he had done. This would be a great offense to the "ones above." Besides, he usually had witnesses. While one did not lie about these things, a little artistic exaggeration was permissible. It made the telling more lively and interesting.

Among some tribes a young warrior would start out with his feathers flat against his head. In time his war honors would make the feathers "stand up" like those of a chief. Four coups were sometimes sufficient to make a man a leader or subchief. Streaming war bonnets were rare. It took a lifetime of great deeds to earn the right to wear one. It was also very dangerous to display one in battle, as all the hostile warriors would vie with each other for the honor of downing such a distinguished enemy or capturing the war bonnet as a trophy. Some men amassed an amazing number of war honors. Red Cloud, the great Sioux leader, counted over eighty coups.

From earliest childhood, Plains Indian boys were brought up to be

The Indians of the Plains were often described as the finest light cavalry in the world. Their feats of horsemanship were legendary. They could hook one leg over the horse's back, letting the animal's body shield their own, discharging their arrows over the pony's neck with deadly accuracy . . . and all this at full gallop.

warriors. Old age, so they were told, was all aches and pains, feebleness and failing eyesight. Much better to die a warrior's death, while one was still young and in the bloom of life. Thus a boy joined his first war party in his early teens. Sometimes he sneaked away without telling his family. He would carry water or cook for the older warriors who had permitted him to come along. They, in turn, would try to protect him and bring him home safely. But they would also give him an opportunity to distinguish himself if circumstances were favorable.

What a fuss a proud father made when a son came home from his first raid. Often he would send the crier out to invite everybody to a big feast in honor of his boy. Then he would give away ponies and other valuable gifts to the poor to celebrate the event, while the women would sing Brave Heart songs, ending in trilling high-pitched cries which made the boy shiver with pride and joy.

For a war party to be a success, the "medicine" had to be good. It was considered to be good if, for example, a man had a favorable dream or vision. These were sometimes very explicit. A man would confidently foretell the capture of exactly sixteen horses or the slaying of a hunchbacked enemy riding a gray pony. The lucky dreamer would call out to his friends: "Warriors, I had a strong dream last night. I went to war against the Pawnee. The signs are good. I must go. Let us have a big party now. Let the crier shout the news, that all may know!"

If a man had many successful raids to his credit, he did not find it hard to get a war party together, because everybody knew that his medicine was good. He would automatically become the leader of the party, which would sometimes be made up only of the members of a certain warrior society.

Good dreams were not enough to assure the favorable outcome of a raid. Each warrior had his own luck-bringing medicine bag. The leader often carried particularly powerful charms, such as the sacred bundle of his warrior society. Sometimes the personal medicine bag of a very famous leader could be bought or borrowed for the enterprise. Some medicine was even supposed to influence the weather, creating fogs and storms that would make pursuit by the enemy impossible.

Broken treaties, the coming of settlers and miners, and the building of roads and forts brought on the great Indian wars in the third quarter of the nineteenth century. This old engraving shows warriors on the warpath. War parties were not usually as large as the one shown here.

However, nobody would hold it against a man if he stayed home, or even left a battle already in progress, because of a bad vision or an evil omen. Nobody would be foolish enough to fight on a day when his medicine was bad.

The young warriors painted themselves carefully with hailstorm patterns which would, so they believed, make it impossible for their enemies to hit them. Special designs painted on a war shirt would protect its wearer against arrows and, after the coming of the white man, against bullets. The skin of a kingfisher tied to a horse's mane

Today the Indian warrior, having fought on the battlefields of Europe, Korea, and Vietnam, often returns to the poverty, the unemployment, and the tarpaper shacks of his reservation.

would give the horse extra speed—"make it fly as swiftly as a bird."

The bravest of all warriors were the sashwearers, the "Fighting Crazies." These included some members of the Sioux Strong Heart Society, the Kit Foxes, and the Cheyenne Dog Soldiers, who wore a long, red strip of cloth slung across their breasts and trailing behind them. When they dismounted during a battle and pinned their sashes to the ground with a stick, they meant: "On this spot I will fight until I am killed or until a friend releases me by pulling the pin out."

A returning war party signaled the success of a raid by waving their blankets and circling their horses. They blackened their faces if they had taken scalps. These were attached to hoops or sticks and given to the women to dance with. Sometimes the warriors would play a trick on their village and come home wailing and pretending to have been beaten. This would make the victory songs sound sweeter, after the joke was discovered. Indian warfare was a glorious sport. The fact that one could get killed playing it only added zest to the game.

Undistinguished and stingy men, bad fighters or hunters, were not invited to join the warrior's society. "Such men just live," said a brave old warrior. It was really the worst one could say about anybody.

Today's Indian warriors fight for Uncle Sam. They are serving in the armed forces in higher numbers in proportion to the Indian population than any other group in the United States. Indian soldiers are known for their bravery and marksmanship; their chests are full of ribbons and medals.

Today, as in the past, there is often a give-away party for a son returning from the army, especially from overseas. Only now the father is apt to give away a transistor radio or a TV set instead of a horse. Soldiers coming back from a shooting war—such as World War II or Korea—are given a scalp dance, without scalps of course.

In the old days, a man coming back from war found a well-defined place in his tribe. He was honored and taken care of even when his fighting days were over. Today the warrior returns to the poverty, tarpaper shacks, and toppling privies of his reservation. No job waits for him. The Pima Indian Ira Hayes, the hero of Iwo Jima, pawned his Congressional Medal of Honor and died in a ditch, unwanted and unemployed. We have invited the Indian to share the burden of our wars, but we have not as yet invited him to share with us the fruits of peace.

7 ▪ GROWING UP

Ho! Sun, moon and stars,
All you that move in the
heavens, listen to me!
Into your midst
new life has come.
Make its path smooth.

Ho! Winds, clouds and rain,
you that move in the air.
Into your midst
new life has come.
Make its path smooth!

OMAHA PRAYER ON THE
BIRTH OF A CHILD

The Plains Indians had a saying that a man's most precious possession is not his horses, his weapons, or his fine tepee, but his children.

The birth of a child was always a joyous event. It was usually the grandmother who bathed and rubbed the baby down with warm buffalo cow fat. The umbilical cord would be preserved and sewn into a small hide bag shaped like a lizard or a turtle and covered with beads. These two creatures were symbols of long life and endurance. The small bag was therefore a powerful good-luck charm which would protect the baby. Usually it was fastened to the cradleboard. As soon as possible the baby was given a name. This would be kept until the baby was big enough to get a grown-up name. From the very first days, a Cheyenne or Sioux mother would gently pinch a baby's nostrils to stifle any cries. A screaming baby was a danger because sound could attract enemies. This was particularly important for the isolated camp of a hunting family. In

An Indian child's ties to his grandparents are very strong. Uncles, aunts, and especially grandmothers are always ready to help take care of the little ones.

this way even tiny infants made their first contribution to their tribe's welfare—they kept quiet.

Small babies were often carried on their mother's back, enfolded within her blanket and warmed by her body. An infant spent most

Children fit naturally into the life of their family and tribe and are not excluded from the world of the grown-ups. They take part in religious ceremonies.

of its first year securely strapped to a cradleboard. Some dry and absorbent plants, such as certain mosses, were used for diapers. Preparing meals for her family, the mother frequently stopped and reached over her shoulder to stuff a particularly delicious morsel into her baby's mouth.

When a tribe was on the move, cradleboards were slung on the mothers' saddlehorns, tied to the end of a lodgepole, or placed

upon a travois. The two "horns" of the cradleboard, together with a broad hoop of wood, protected the baby's soft head from injury in case a horse bolted and threw the cradleboard to the ground. The cradleboard was always beautifully decorated with beads and porcupine quills, a proud mother's chief exhibit of her skill with a needle.

Indian children were quiet and well-behaved. They were seldom punished and never beaten or screamed at. They were asked to do something, not told. Children were never alone. They knew they were loved. Besides his own parents, there were always grandfathers and uncles to help bring up a boy, grandmothers and aunts to watch over a girl. With so many people concerned with his welfare, a child had no chance to become a "mamma's boy."

Children were encouraged to learn to walk, ride, and swim at an early age. They acquired knowledge and skills by trying to imitate those older than themselves. They had toys and played games. Many of their games trained them into their tribal roles. Little girls played house, or rather tepee, setting up little tents which their mothers had made and painted for them. Little boys pretended to be hunters bringing home game, a tiny buffalo carved in wood or a toy elk made of skin stuffed with grass, which they used as a target for their children's bows. Sometimes they even managed to kill a rabbit with their toy weapons. How proud they were then! Boys imitated grown-up warriors by striking coup upon a piece of meat hanging on a drying rack, carrying it off in triumph as if it were a stolen horse.

Youngsters made blowguns out of hollowed ash stems. There were many exciting ball games that boys and girls could play. One could also always have a good mudball fight.

As the boys grew bigger, they used larger and larger bows, took care of the horses, and went along on the hunt until they finally brought down their first buffalo calf. This was a moment to be remembered.

"Look at all this good meat my son has brought!" cried the happy father as he prepared a feast in honor of the big event. The Indians were wise in the ways of building up a youngster's confidence and feeling of importance. Maybe the boy would be given the tongue, which was the best part. The meat was often given away, together with many other fine things, to impress upon the youngster the great virtue of generosity and responsibility for the welfare of others.

At last the day came when a boy was ready to become a man. The Plains Indian was a vision seeker. Dreams and images, seen only in his mind's eye, were his way of communicating with the Great Spirit. To gain the vision which he needed to become a man, a boy faced an ordeal of loneliness, hunger, and thirst—trials which would test his bravery and courage.

Humbly he asked a strong and wise man, a relative if possible, to help him. First they prepared a sweat lodge. This was done with

At a sun dance at Rosebud, South Dakota, this young boy danced with the grown men.

Hoop dancers start young. They have to be agile enough to keep eight or ten hoops in motion at the same time.

great care according to an age-old ritual. Every step had its symbolic meaning. Willow sticks were stuck in the ground and bent to form a small, circular hut. This framework was covered with buffalo skins. Nowadays quilted blankets are used.

At the entrance a sacred pipe was placed, its stem pointing upwards as a sign that the earth and heavens were now joined in harmony. The boy and his helper entered the hut and stripped to their breech-cloths. Outside, a number of large stones were heated in a blazing fire. One by one they were brought into the sweat lodge on a forked stick. The entrance was covered up and cold water was poured over the glowing stones. At once, the little hut was filled with hot, white steam, the "breath of life." The boy was given as much water as he could drink. As the sweat streamed from his pores, his body was cleansed of all impurities. Now he was prepared to receive his vision.

His helper guided him to a lonely and secluded place on top of a hill. He looked for a tree or rock against which the boy could lean when he became weak. Or he placed him in a "vision pit," a hole dug into the ground. He might press a sacred pipe into the boy's hand to give him comfort and courage. Then he would leave him. The vision quests were not undertaken during the winter when a boy would have frozen to death during a blizzard.

The boy remained on his lonely hilltop, stripped naked, without food or water, exposed to the sun and the cold of the night. As he grew faint with hunger, his body seemed strangely light and his mind opened to the voices and whisperings from above. In a state of half-wakefulness, he waited for his vision to come to him. Cut off from the everyday world, huddled in the vision pit, or cowering naked under a buffalo hide, surrounded by the velvet darkness of the night, the boy endured his lonely vigil. The cry of a straying animal or the rustling wind were the only sounds which penetrated the stillness about him.

Soon he lost all sense of time and space. How grateful he was if his helper came up once a day for a brief moment to hear how he was faring, saying "One day is already gone" or "Two days are gone by

Among the Sioux, men undergo a vision quest, fasting for as long as four days and nights in an underground cave—the so-called vision pit. The first fast, which takes place when a boy is in his late teens, is often his initiation into manhood.

now!" But the helper did not always do this. After three or four long days and nights, when the boy had had his vision, the helper brought him back to the camp, where he was fed and warmed.

His helper, who was wise and compassionate, listened carefully as the boy told him of his dreams. He would ask the boy about the animals he had seen or heard, because this was important. He would also help to interpret the dreams whose meanings were not always clear.

An Indian's initiation into manhood was a momentous event in his life. His vision gave him his adult name. If, for instance, he had dreamed about an elk, then "Elk" would be part of his name. His first medicine bundle was made up according to what he had heard, seen, or imagined during his long fast. Thus his vision often shaped his future. He would faithfully try to live up to it.

Sitting Bull had a vision that he would be a great medicine man, responsible for the welfare of his people, and he made it come true. Likewise, Crazy Horse dreamed that he must scorn honors, wealth, and fine clothing, ignore insults and small matters, and dedicate himself to the defense of his tribe. He lived according to his dream.

If a young vision seeker happened to be a Sioux, and if he dreamed of thunder or the thunder beings, his whole life changed abruptly. His vision made him into a heyoka, a "contrarywise," a "backwards-forwards man." On one side of his head his hair was shaved, on the other side it fell below his waist. He wore his clothes and moccasins backwards, so that he was coming at the same time he was going. He rode his horse backwards, too, his face toward the tail and his back toward the front.

He always said the opposite of what he meant and did the opposite of what was demanded. Instead of "yes" he said "no." In an icy wind he pretended to be suffering a sunstroke. In the heat of a summer day he lay shivering under a mountain of blankets, pretending to be cold. In these strange ways a heyoka amused and comforted his people. A heyoka's appearance made people smile. Indians have always been aware that life and truth have two faces—one is sad and one is funny, but it is really only one face which keeps changing forever. A heyoka used his great mystic powers for the people, as he had a gift of curing the sick.

If he grew tired of his role as a sacred clown and wished to become, once more, a normal person, he had to plunge his bare arms into a boiling kettle of dog meat and take out the head. This was the only way to stop being an "upside-down man."

A man could fast and seek dreams whenever he felt that his life was at a turning point. He could also change his name again, as a result of a memorable deed, but nothing could equal the impact of his first vision which made him a man.

A few men, a very few, did not want to lead the competitive, dangerous life of a warrior. These men, called *berdaches* by French trappers, simply put on women's clothing and did women's work. They did not fight. Nobody objected or made fun of them. A person had to act according to his dreams and visions. What he did with his life was his own business.

Nowadays, only a few full-blooded parents still cling to their ancient beliefs and send their sons to a lonely hill to seek a vision. This is done most often in a medicine man's family.

Girls were as important to their parents and to their tribe as the boys, but they did not have to undergo a lonely vigil without food or water in order to attain womanhood. When a girl became physically old enough to be a mother, her parents would announce a feast in her honor. They would give her new, beautiful clothes and other gifts. She would be paraded around the camp circle while her elder relatives made speeches about what a fine young woman she was. They would praise her skill in sewing and tanning. For a girl, coming of age was a proud moment.

Indian childhood was a happy childhood. Children were precious because the tribe was small and the life of the hunter full of danger. Each young life was very important and the love shown to the little ones reflected this importance.

Today, Indian children are still treated with this kind of love, but the modern world has brought its own problems. Indian children, like all others, have to go to school. Teachers are mostly white. They do not speak the Indian languages and, from the point of view of the pupils, seem to come from a different world. Learning is not easy for a child who cannot understand his teacher. The schoolbooks, too, do not always make sense to young Indians. These books depict white families in suburban homes. They show daddy coming home from his office on the commuter train. The Indian child, living in an isolated cabin among lonely hills, cannot relate to this.

Some reservations are huge and sparsely populated. The government can't build schools for each tiny settlement with its small handful of children. So it builds a few huge boarding schools which must serve a number of areas and communities. This may be the practical thing to do, but it causes great hardship to the Indian children who are taken from their homes to a faraway school, where they have to face a new kind of life among strangers and have to manage for themselves without the help of parents and grown-up relatives.

A Cheyenne grandfather says: "They built this new boarding school over there. All glass and stone. Very modern, very beautiful, very expensive. But the kids in there! Some of them commit suicide. They aren't used to being by themselves, without their families. They don't have enough love. Nobody understands."

"White people don't make good parents," explains a young Sioux mother. "On the one hand they spoil the kids, make things too easy for them, overprotect them, so that it takes the youngster a long time to grow up. On the other hand they slap them and yell at them."

Indian parents are not forever saying, "Don't touch, be careful!" They let the children discover, at the price of a little hurt, that they should stay away from fire and sharp things.

A white teacher at Pine Ridge reads from a schoolbook designed for Sioux children: "In the old buffalo-hunting days, everybody had to share their food and their possessions or the tribe would perish. Bravery, today, is saying 'no' to your relative who asks you for a hand-out. Bravery, today, is looking out for your own, immediate family. Bravery, today, is punching the time clock at 8 A.M. in the factory."

An Indian teen-age girl comments on this: "Maybe, instead of telling us this, you should teach white children how to share, how to say 'yes' to the poor, how not to punch the time clock."

A young Sioux mother summed it all up: "In the old days you had to be brave, even the children. You had to watch out all the time— for grizzly bears, Crow, and the U.S. Cavalry. But today, to grow up now, that takes real courage. With all the problems we have, every Indian child today has to be as brave as Crazy Horse or Sitting Bull."

8 ▪ THE SOUND OF FLUTES

You may go
on the warpath.
When your name I hear
having done
something brave.
Then, I will marry you.

SIOUX LOVE SONG

A Mandan woman's value is:
Two horses, a gun with
powder and ball for a year;
5 or 6 pounds of beads
and a couple of gallons
of whisky.

GEORGE CATLIN

A young man once heard a strange, rattling noise. As he looked about him, he discovered a woodpecker hammering on a dead branch. The bird seemed to say, "Come here, come here!" The young man walked over to the spot and the bird flew away. The man saw that the woodpecker had drilled a row of holes in the dead branch. As a gust of wind blew through them, the branch made a wonderful sound such as the young man had never heard before. He broke it off and discovered that it was hollow. Blowing into the branch while running his fingers over the holes, the young man found that he could play a melody. He took the piece of wood home. This was the first flute. Because the woodpecker had shown it to him, the young man carved one end into the shape of a bird's head with an open beak. Most Plains Indian flutes still look this way.

Flutes are made for the playing of love songs only. The wailing of one of these instruments told the people that a young man had lost

For the Plains Indian the sound of a flute was a message of love. Young men, too shy to express their feelings for a girl in words, let the flute speak for them.

his heart to a girl. A flute could convey messages, such as "I am waiting for you" or "Meet me tomorrow." Indians were shy and bashful lovers. A brave young warrior who had already counted coup often did not have the courage to speak to the girl of his choice. He let the flute do the talking.

Not that there weren't enough opportunities for meeting her. A girl's first chore upon getting up in the morning was to go to the river with her skin bag to fetch water. Water that had been left in its container overnight was considered "dead water." The path that led from the camp to the river was a good place to meet one's girl. As she came up the path with her full water bag, a boy might just accidentally be leaning against a cottonwood tree. Often the admirer was tongue-tied, seemingly preoccupied with some trivial task, such as whittling. In return he got a sidelong glance, and that was all. He could also hide behind a bush and shoot an arrow through her water bag. This might make her angry, but it could also make her laugh. At least she had to take notice of him.

Cheyenne boys had still another way of "getting acquainted." It was a girl's job to dig for turnips and to gather berries, just as it was a young man's job to go hunting. Cheyenne girls liked to make up root digging parties. As they came back with their loads, the girls would find their way barred by a group of young warriors. This was a good chance to play the "come and try to take our turnips away" game. The turnips were laid on the ground. The girls defended them by pelting the men with clumps of earth, sticks of dry wood, or buffalo chips. A girl could make it easy for a boy to "strike coup" upon a load of turnips. That was one way of saying "I like you."

An Indian girl would look for a strong man, who was both a good hunter who could provide his family with plenty of meat, and a brave warrior who could protect them. If he was also handsome, so much the better. Plains Indians were vain in their appearance and they wanted to look their best when they went courting. They were very much concerned with cleanliness. Both men and women bathed daily. An Indian's day usually started with a plunge into the nearest river.

After a swim, unless there was something special to do, it was time to dress up in one's best clothes. Catlin described a warrior in all his finery:

"His pride had plumed and tinted him in all the freshness and brilliance of an Indian garment. He was dressed in his native costume, which was classic and exceedingly beautiful; his leggings and shirt were of mountain goat skin, richly garnished with quills from the porcupine and fringed with the locks of scalps taken from his enemies' heads. His head was decked with the war eagle's plumes, his robe was of the skin of a young buffalo bull, decorated with battle scenes."

Indian flutes are shaped like a bird's head with an open beak.

Young men were also proud of their long hair and spent much time and care on it. The Cree brushed it with the rough side of a buffalo's tongue. The Crow, who had the longest hair of all—so long that it sometimes reached to the ground—used porcupine bristles for combing it.

The young Indian man, on the other hand, looked for a modest virtuous girl, skilled in tanning and beading, one who would be a good wife and mother. He was, to be quite frank about it, looking for a workhorse. Working or not, a girl had to look attractive. Women spent no less time than men on their appearance. The gala dress of a

Crow lady was studded with three hundred elk teeth. As only two particular teeth of each animal were used, such a garment was very expensive. A hundred teeth were the price of one good horse.

Girls were carefully educated for their roles in life. A Blackfoot father spent some time making his daughter into a poised, desirable woman, not a giddy, giggling little thing. He would take her aside when she was still quite young, tell her funny stories, roll his eyes, wiggle his ears, and act just plain silly. If his daughter burst out giggling, he would tell her to go ahead and to laugh as much and as long as she wanted. When she calmed down at last, he would repeat the performance. He would keep this up for days until, at last, she could keep a straight face. "Now you are acting like a fine, young woman," he would say then, and this part of her education would be over.

Indians loved sport and games, as this Catlin painting, depicting a girls' ball game, shows.

This girl from the Crow tribe wears a dress covered with elk teeth. As only two teeth from each animal are used, such a dress is a girl's most prized possession.

After the first bashful "boy meets girl" games, the "chance" meetings at the river, the flute playing from afar, it was time, at last, to be seriously thinking of marriage. The form of courtship was dictated by the conditions of life. There was little privacy in an Indian village, and no privacy at all in the tepee. Young lovers seldom went out into the prairie to be by themselves, because this was very dangerous. In case of an enemy raid, the boy would be hampered by having to protect the girl and both were likely to be killed. For this reason, a special form of courtship evolved.

The Indians had a way of creating privacy where none existed. The girl would stand in front of her family's tepee with a blanket. The suitor would step up to her and she would wrap the blanket around both of them, making sure that their heads were covered. Enfolded thus, standing face to face, they were "alone," free to whisper sweet nothings and endearments. Being in the blanket meant not being there at all. Friends and relatives pretended not to see the couple standing in the blanket. They knew how not to intrude. A girl could stand in her blanket with more than one suitor in one evening, talking to them, getting acquainted. In this way, she made her choice. This was the approved, respectable way of finding your husband. In a few tribes this "courting in a blanket" was not done, but a grandmother would act as a go-between for two lovers. She would carry their messages and receive a horse for her services.

Indian marriage ceremonies were very simple. The Cheyenne bride, together with a bundle of gifts, would be placed on a blanket and carried to the lodge of the groom's father. If the parents of the young couple were wealthy enough to furnish them with a tepee, the young people might start out with a household of their own. Generally, however, they moved into their parents' lodge, most often the wife's parents. Among Plains Indians, a man usually moved in with his wife's family. If his wife belonged to another tribe, he would be adopted into her people, unless he had captured her in war.

The fact that a future husband gave a number of horses and other gifts to the girl's family gave many white people the idea that the Indian woman was a slave, who could be bought like cattle. This was not true. The gifts were a mark of respect to show what high regard the young man had for his bride. Often he would hunt for food for her parents to make up for a lack of gifts. It was also customary for the woman's family to make presents in return, usually of value equal to those received.

The prairie was very much a man's world because a tribe survived by hunting and warfare, which were men's occupations. Still, women had many rights and were respected members of the tribe. A man was conscious of the fact that even the proudest warrior could not exist without the help of a woman. A woman ruled in the tepee. She had a right to her own property. She gained honor through her activities. Winning against her competitors in a crafts contest was like the counting of a coup by a warrior. Women had their own sports, and in some games they competed with men on an equal basis. A man who mistreated his wife had to face the anger of her relatives. There was an unwritten law which protected the weak and the helpless, and a man who broke it was shamed before the whole tribe. In a severe case he might even be driven from the village.

A new couple fell in naturally with the rhythm of village life, which was one of the sharing chores. The wife was responsible for putting up the tepee, which in some tribes was her personal property. The husband was supposed to provide the lodgepoles. After the man had killed and butchered an animal, the woman took over the hide and scraped, and tanned, and sewed. She would challenge the other women to a quilling and beading contest, sending the crier around with her invitation. Among the settled tribes it was the woman who planted the squash and the corn, tended the field, and reaped the harvest. This made the proud, nomadic Sioux and Cheyenne say, "Our women are pretty and walk well; they are not stooped and gnarled from hoeing corn."

As a man grew older and assumed more responsibilities, he often took another wife. Sometimes he had three or four. This is not as strange as it sounds. It has, as a matter of fact, a very simple explanation. A warrior and hunter was in constant danger. He could be, and often was, killed by an enemy, or he might be gored by a buffalo. So, there were always many more women than men in a tribe. The Indians did not think it good or charitable that a woman should be unprovided for, without a husband or children. Orphans often lived in a man's lodge, helping to take care of his horses and doing chores. No widow or lone child went unprovided for.

There was still another reason for a man to have more than one

Many Plains Indian women are skilled bead-workers, decorating head bands, belts, and moccasins with traditional colorful designs.

wife. As a warrior rose to be a chief, he had to take care of many more people. It was expected that he would be generous and hospitable. He had to give many feasts and presents. Therefore, one wife could not possibly do all the beading, tanning, and cooking necessary to keep up her husband's position. A considerate man would then say, "I must take another wife. My old one is not strong enough to do all this work by herself." Sometimes the wife, herself, suggested this. A man would then usually marry his wife's younger sister. That way there was very little jealousy. To the grumbling early missionaries, a chief would point out that Abraham, Isaac, and Jacob, too, had had more than one wife. At least so he had been told. The patriarchs of the Bible had, after all, led lives that were in many ways similar to those of the Plains Indians.

It was a life which certainly suited the men. They were exposed to danger daily; they hunted and they fought. Little else was expected from them in the way of work.

Certainly, the women did practically all the work. Without this work the tribal life would have fallen apart. But a woman also could become famous as a medicine woman and healer. A spirited, strong-hearted girl could, if she felt like it, ride with the men into battle and fight alongside them.

During the battle on the Rosebud River, in which the combined Sioux and Cheyenne defeated General George Crook, Buffalo Calf Road Woman rode with the warriors. When her brother, Chief Comes-in-Sight, had his horse killed under him, she dashed into the midst of the battle, right among the blue-coated "Long Knives," and her brother mounted behind her on the horse. Then she galloped cooly back to her own lines, and the warriors stopped their fighting long enough to let out a long, mighty yell of admiration for the brave girl. To the Indians this battle has always been known as the "Fight where the girl saved her brother."

At a modern powwow in Montana, women are busy preparing a "Big Feed."

Today, Plains Indian men are no longer the undisputed rulers of their families that they were long ago. Men are in charge of tribal politics and religious ceremonies, but it is sometimes a woman who rules the man, who rules the tribal council. It is no longer possible for a man to be just a hunter or warrior. He has to work on the road, in the field, on a ranch, or in a factory. Often his wife and daughters work beside and with him.

Boys and girls receive the same education. Many young people leave the reservation to study in a college or to go to the cities to find work. Within a tribe it is often easier for a woman than a man to get a government job as a nurse's aid, teacher, secretary, or bookkeeper. Women also earn money with their crafts, such as moccasin making and beadwork.

In some families it is the mother who takes care of business, who negotiates with the Bureau of Indian Affairs on such matters as lease money or commodity foods, because men find such dealings not to their taste. All this means that Indian women take a bigger part in the affairs of their communities, go to meetings, and let their views be known. The Plains Indians' world used to be a man's world, but this is no longer true today.

9 ▪ THE GIVE-AWAY PARTY

Oh! How I love a people
who don't live for
the love of money!

GEORGE CATLIN

George Catlin once summed up his feelings of friendship and admiration for the Indians in one short and moving paragraph: "I love a people who have always made me welcome to the best they had, who are honest without laws, who have no jails and no poorhouse, who worship God without a Bible—and I believe that God loves them also—who have never raised a hand against me, or stolen my property, where there was no law to punish either, and oh! How I love a people who don't live for the love of money!"

Catlin's views were not shared by the government people in Washington. He was an artist and therefore, in their opinion, impractical and muddleheaded, full of romantic notions. The government people had never been to the Plains, and they had, for the most part, never seen an Indian. But they were very sure that they knew what was wrong with him—the trouble with the Indian was that he was not selfish enough.

In 1851 the Secretary of the Interior put it this way: "To tame the savage you must tie him down to the soil. You must make him understand the value of property, and the benefits of its separate ownership. You must appeal to those selfish principles implanted by divine providence in the nature of man for the wisest purposes."

Among whites a man acquires stature by amassing wealth. His fine house and his expensive car parked in the driveway proclaim to the world "I am a success." Among Indians, however, a man earns

Many tribes held a special "Beggar's Dance"; this was an appeal to the
Great Spirit to open the heart of the rich, so that they would give—not
to the dancers, but to the poor.

the respect of his tribe by giving things away. The fine horse he gives
to a poor person proclaims "I care!" Among whites, a man saves
money to leave to his wife and children. But among Indians, a dead
man's possessions were given to the needy. The pass them on to one's
sons would only prevent them from obtaining horses by their own
brave deeds. It might have made them too lazy to get their own
buffalo robes by hunting. Generosity was the Plains peoples' greatest
virtue. It ranked even before bravery and hunting skill. An Indian's
happiness was to give, to provide for the helpless ones.

Many tribes held a special "beggars" dance, which was an appeal
to the Great Spirit to open the hearts of the rich ones, that they
should give, not to the dancers, but to the poor of the tribe.
There is no more unfair expression than the term *Indian giver*.

George Catlin told how he tried to buy a beautiful pair of decorated leggings from a Mandan brave. The man stubbornly refused to sell them, even for a horse. When Catlin finally left for home, with everybody knowing that he would be gone forever, the young Mandan suddenly appeared, trotting briskly along the river, and threw a package into Catlin's boat. He waved a last farewell and rode off. It took Catlin a while to untie the many knots of the rawhide bundle. Inside he found the leggings he had tried to buy. The Indian had made a gift of something he would not sell to Catlin. What's more, he had arranged things so that it was impossible for Catlin to make him a present in return or even to thank him. To give without embarrassing or humiliating the receiver was as important as the gift itself.

Charity extended beyond the tribe. In the winter of 1875–76, U.S. troops attacked a Cheyenne village. The Cheyenne were not at war with the whites, and their camp was not guarded. They fled from their tepees naked, as they had slept, the women clutching the little ones, the warriors defending them as best as they could with a few hastily snatched-up weapons. The Cheyennes lost everything: their tepees, their blankets, their clothes, their stores of meat. Naked they made their way through snow and icy winds to a Sioux camp.

Chief Woodenlegs described what happened then: "From every Sioux tepee came shouts: "Cheyennes, come and eat here!" Sioux women cooked more and more steaming meat. The Sioux crier rode through the camp, calling out so that all could hear: "The Cheyennes are very poor. All who have blankets or robes or tepees to spare should give to them!" Soon the camp circle was thronged with men and women eagerly bringing all that they could spare. "Who needs a blanket?"—"I do."—"Take this one!" "Who wants a tepee?"— "Give it to me!"—"It is yours." "Who wants a horse?"—"I do!"— "Ride this one!" In no time at all, the Cheyennes had everything

Being a Plains Indian means sharing your food with others. There are many give-away feasts at which all comers are fed—provided they bring their own dishes. A give-away feast means cooking and baking by the whole community, tables covered with food, many smiling faces. Everyone lines up and has a good time. After the meal the dancing begins.

they needed to set up a new village. The help given to them by the Sioux is still gratefully remembered by the Cheyenne today.

The government official who appealed to the Indians' "selfish interests" over a hundred years ago did so in vain. The sharing and the give-away parties are still going on, as always. Visitors watching an Indian powwow may not be aware that the loudspeaker is not announcing a new dance, but that someone is giving a pot of coffee to the drummers or that someone else is giving away a pickup truck in gratitude for his son's recovery from a car accident.

The Indian way of sharing often comes into conflict with the "sound business practices" of the white community. It is hard to be an Indian and a good businessman at the same time. When one is living off the reservation, away from the tribal unit, the simple community unit of the tribe comes into direct conflict with the complex world of the white man.

A Sioux lady, living in an industrial town off the reservation, bought a small apartment house from which she planned to make a living. The apartments were quickly rented by poor Indian families. It turned out that they could not pay the rent. The landlady also found out that her tenants had no money for food or doctor bills, so she had to take a job to provide for them. But she didn't mind; everybody loved her.

Another Indian, having worked for years at a good job in California, came back to the reservation. With his life savings, he opened a gas station. He was elected to the office of tribal president. Every day many cars lined up at his gasoline pump. "You are a big man now," the drivers would say to him, "surely you won't charge us poor folks for a little gas?" Soon the man was broke, his savings gone, but for years afterwards he will be remembered as a chief who took care of his people.

Still another Indian opened a cafeteria. Many poor families came there to eat. The owner did not have the heart to ask them to pay. But this man did not go broke. He hired a white waiter. He spread the rumor that he had sold the cafeteria to him, that the waiter was the new owner. After that only people with enough money to pay for their meals went to the cafeteria. The poor ones stayed away. They knew that a white man would not feed them.

Today, more and more young white people come to the reservations. They are searching for something, a philosophy of life which they cannot find in their own cities. Perhaps they will find that the Indians' great gift of unselfish sharing is an expression of true humanity which has been lacking in their home communities.

10 ▪ ORDER WITHOUT LAW

*The Indians are
all gentlemen.*

FATHER DE SMET

*The fascinating combination
of stoical heroism and priestly
bearing gave the Indians of the
Plain something of the majesty
of the eagle and the sun.*

FRITJOF SCHUON

Among a people without locks, keys, or money, there were no thieves. Warriors stole horses from their enemies, but of these deeds of war a man could be proud. Without lawyers, contracts, or anything in print, men found it impossible to cheat. Without jails there could be no criminals. The tribes of the Plains had no caste system, no classes, no inherited leadership, no underdogs. One man was as good as another.

A chief remained a chief only by wise leadership and lavish generosity. He had no power to punish. He could not raise his hand against the meanest member of the tribe.

In the democracies of the Plains, every member of the tribe had his say. In a tribal council, he would be listened to respectfully and without interruption. It did not matter how long he spoke—there was plenty of time. Only if he did not speak to the point would the crier knock on the floor with his staff to remind him to stick to the subject.

The Plains Indians loved a public debate and were proud of their speeches. They could not understand why the whites complained

In the democratic society of the Plains, every member of the tribe had his say. In a tribal council he would be listened to respectfully and without interruption.

of their long-windedness. A good, long speech was fine entertainment. In this way matters of importance were settled by common consent. Men with opposite views had a chance to express them fully. As there were no cuss words in the Indian's language, men found it hard to insult each other.

The society of the Plains Indian was an open society in the truest sense of the term. Indians could have no secrets, nor could they hide their deeds. There was no punishment if they did wrong, but they could be shamed into behaving properly. If nothing else helped, a man could be made into an object of ridicule. Jokes would be told about him and the women would laugh at him.

This was law enforcement without jail. Sometimes there was bad blood between two men, and, in anger, one of them would kill the other. Before people went crazy with drinking the white man's whiskey, this happened very rarely. The killing of a tribal brother was the worst thing that could befall a tribe. The sacred bundles in the medicine lodge had to be repurified. The whole tribe had to cleanse itself of the deed. The killer's relatives went to the victim's family offering to pay for his life with everything they possessed. The killer sometimes offered himself as a substitute provider and protector.

Among the Cheyenne a murderer was banned from tribal activities for four years. During this time he had to live outside the village, without a tepee or a pipe. Nobody spoke to him. One such outcast, helped by his immediate family, saved his tribe by wiping out an enemy war party. But this act did not shorten his exile.

Many times the law of the Plains Indian was unwritten and unenforced—except by his own conscience.

Little Wolf was one of the greatest leaders the Cheyenne ever had. After the Custer fight, his people were forcibly removed from their old hunting grounds in Montana and put on a reservation in Oklahoma. This was a fever-ridden place where nothing grew and mosquitoes were the only crop. There they were left to starve, to sicken, and to die of malaria. When the government refused their many desperate pleas to be allowed to leave that death trap, Little

Wolf led his people. "Permission or no permission," he said, "we are going home!"

Home was more than a thousand miles away. More than ten thousand soldiers barred the way. Little Wolf's tiny band consisted mostly of women and children. The handful of warriors were, for the most part, unarmed. There were not enough horses. Four times the Cheyennes had to fight their way through the lines of the soldiers. Little Wolf's march of desperation, through hostile country in the midst of a cold winter, was one of the greatest feats in the annals of American history. It was successful insofar as the survivors were eventually permitted to once again live in their old homeland where a reservation was created for them.

Reservation life did not agree with Little Wolf and he started drinking. During a drunken brawl he killed a man. He never forgave himself. He wore only the meanest clothes. He gave up the pleasure of smoking. He never spoke again in the council of chiefs. He lived voluntarily as an outcast until the day he died.

Sometimes, the conflict between the white man's law and the unwritten codes of the Indians worked to an Indian's advantage. When Crow Dog shot his rival, the famous chief Spotted Tail, he was brought to trial in Deadwood City, and everybody expected him to be hanged. But his lawyer pointed out that there was no law which forbade one Indian to kill another. And so Crow Dog went free.

More often than not, the law worked against the Indian. While white citizens enjoyed complete freedom of religion under the Constitution, Indians were jailed for practicing their old beliefs. After the 1930s, matters improved, but the white man's laws are still a problem.

"There are over 2,000 laws and statutes governing Indians," said a

Chief Lame Deer, a Sioux medicine man, planted a sacred staff on Mount Rushmore and said a peacepipe prayer to remind people that the Black Hills are still sacred to the Indians.

former tribal president. "It's a real jungle of laws and only a very few experts can find their way through it."

"The law is supposed to treat everybody the same," added Chief Lame Deer, from Winner, South Dakota, "but it doesn't work out that way. Here in town, when a white man gets drunk, they handle

In the summer of 1970, a group of Indians including Chief Lame Deer, Lehman Brightman, and Minnie Bacon, demonstrated on top of Mount Rushmore for Indian rights.

him with kid gloves. The police will bring him home, in their own patrol car, to his old lady. But when an Indian gets drunk, they put him in jail and fine him."

Understanding can come with a little good will on both sides. In the summer of 1970 a group of Indians took over Mount Rushmore National Memorial in the Black Hills, in what amounted to a kind

The sacred Black Hills as seen from the top of Theodore Roosevelt's giant head, where Indians demonstrated for the return of tribal lands.

of sit-in. The Indians were angered by the fact that the government had not given back more than 200,000 acres of land on the Pine Ridge Reservation which had been taken over as a bombing range for the air force during World War II. They were also angry over the discrimination practiced against them in Rapid City, and because they were allowed no concession to sell their arts and crafts within the Mount Rushmore National Park. Occupying it, they hoped, would draw attention to their complaints. People from Pine Ridge and Rapid City took part; old ladies in their sixties, as well as young children. They were joined by Indian civil rights leaders from across the country and by Indian students living off the reservations.

Minnie Bacon, a young Assiniboin student, was one of the demonstrators.

"At first the situation was hairy," she remembers, "there were all these park rangers with their guns, it was dark, everybody was tense. These were *our* sacred Black Hills. It was also *their* National Park. We promised not to be violent and not to deface their monument. They stretched their law a bit and let us stay. They saw our point of view. Now they even deliver our mail. These rangers are all right, most of them. Some of the white tourists don't dig us, though."

Most reservations have their own Indian police force now, and their own tribal courts and judges, which handle all but the most serious offenses. But problems with white police and law enforcement remain. "There is still a wide gulf between your and our idea of what the law should stand for," said a young mother from Rosebud, South Dakota. "We want to live in harmony with our white brothers. We want to have our equal rights under equal laws, but these must be adjusted to our way of life because, most of all, we want to remain Indians!"

11 ▪ THE SPIRIT WORLD

See not only with your two eyes,
but also with the one eye
which is in your heart.

JOHN EPES BROWN

The white man goes into
his church house
and talks about Jesus,
but the Indian goes into
his tepee and talks to Jesus.

CHIEF QUANAH PARKER

The Indian lived forever in a land of mystery. His life was one long, never-ending, religious ceremony. He saw the unseeable and heard voices which only he could understand. Even the simple tasks of his daily life were transformed by him into rites and prayers.

The Indian's church was the open sky, his altar a buffalo skull and a pipe. His god was Wakan Tanka, the Great Spirit who was one but also many. He was visible, yet invisible. Wakan Tanka was the Great Mystery which had no beginning and no end. Sky, Sun, Moon, and Earth were all part of Wakan Tanka, though they were also gods by themselves. So were Thunder and Wind.

The Great Mystery's symbol was the circle. It stood for the Sun and the Earth, the Tepee and the Sacred Hoop of the Nation. As long as the circle was unbroken, the tribes would flourish. The sacred powers always worked in circles. The eagle, a holy messenger of the

This buffalo altar shows the sacred objects used before a religious ceremony: stones to heat the sweatbath, a buffalo skull, a braid of purifying,
aromatic sweet grass, the peace pipe, and a rawhide bag containing
kinnickinnick (red willow bark tobacco). All rites, including the Yuwipi
ceremony, start with a sweatbath in which all of these things are used.

"ones above," describes a wheel in its flight. The wind moves in
round whirls. The sun comes and goes in a circle. If a man is not
aware that he, too, has within himself this sacred center, that he is
part of the mystic circle together with all other living creatures,
then he is not really a man.

Unlike the white man, the Indian met his gods face to face. He needed no priest between himself and the spirit world. Man was the link between earth and sky. He communicated with the Great Spirit through dreams and visions which told him what to do. The Indian worshiped alone and in silence. His religion was a very personal thing. His visions were for himself only and for nobody else. He might invent his own ways to communicate with the "ones above." He tried to convince nobody that his way was the only right way. On the other hand, nobody interfered with his personal beliefs. According to his vision, he made up his medicine bag, which he opened only when he was alone. His medicine bundle and pipe were his own portable church, very much like the ark of the covenant in the Old Testament. The objects in a man's medicine bundle—stones and pebbles, an oddly shaped root, the claws or bones of an animal—as well as his peace pipe, were not mere inanimate things. They had a life of their own and they had great power.

Some men, too, had been given special powers, the gifts of healing and prophecy which they used on behalf of the people. They were called medicine men. There were different kinds of medicine men.

A man could be holy, but he did not have to perform miracles or do anything out of the ordinary. One knew that he had a strange power, a power to do good, which could not be explained but which could be felt by everybody. He was compassionate, he existed and worked for his people. Such a man was Sitting Bull.

The second kind of medicine man was a healer. He was wise in knowledge of herbs and how to use them to cure sick people. Up to a comparatively short time ago, before the appearance of the so-called wonder drugs, herbs could be bought in all pharmacies and drugstores. Our grandmothers bought herbs for headaches and coughs, powdered roots for a stomachache, or teas that would make one sleep. They were effective for simple ailments.

(*Left*) The peace pipe is sacred to all Plains tribes. The red pipestone represents the flesh and blood of the Indians, the smoke the living breath of the Great Spirit.

(*Right*) The Indian worshiped alone and in silence. Raising his pipe in prayer, he formed a living link between grandmother earth and the Great Spirit above.

The medicine men with their herbs were the pharmacists of the Plains. They also used many magic tricks and incantations in their cures. With some sleight-of-hand trick, they would extract porcupine quills, sticks, and lizards from a patient's mouth. These were the sicknesses to be gotten rid of. We should not laugh about this. A modern doctor's bedside manners and gleaming gadgets are also used to reassure the patient and give him confidence to overcome his disease. A man who believes that his doctor has the right touch or a special sixth sense is already half-cured.

Catlin described the Blackfoot medicine man, White Buffalo, this way: "His dress was as strangely a medley and mixture, perhaps, of the mysteries of the animal and vegetable kingdoms that ever was seen. Besides the skins of many animals, which are also abnormalities and deformities, which render them medicine, he also wore the skins of snakes, frogs, and bats—beaks and toes and tails of birds, hoofs of deer and antelopes—in fact the odds and ends, tails and tips of almost everything that swims, flies, or runs in this part of the world."

A third kind of medicine man occurs mainly among the Sioux

tribes. He is the Yuwipi man—the "tied-up one." The Yuwipi man's specialty is to find the cause of a disease, a missing person, a stolen object, or the result of the coming tribal elections. Yuwipi men are still an important part of the Sioux reservation life. To engage the powers of a Yuwipi man, one has only to send him a peace pipe with some tobacco and, nowadays, about twenty dollars worth of food. Most of this is used to feed all the people taking part in the ceremony. The Yuwipi man really has very little choice. If the pipe is properly sent, he has to accept it and perform the ritual.

To perform it properly the medicine man and his helpers and chief participants should first purify themselves with a sweat bath. Then a room has to be specially prepared. First, the furniture which would be in the way is removed. An altar is set up with four flags, or offerings of cloth, in red, white, yellow, and black—symbolizing the four directions, north, south, east, and west. Some men also interpret these colors to represent the four races of mankind. From a staff, half-red and half-black, stuck into a container filled with earth, hangs an eagle feather and a deer tail. In front of the staff is spread the main altar made of earth into which some simple symbolic designs are drawn. Every medicine man has his own design according to his vision. At each side of the altar is placed a rattle—a gourd filled with small pebbles. A long, thin string, into which many small bundles of tobacco have been tied, is unrolled and laid out in the form of a square. Imagine that the room contained a large rug. Then the sacred line would run around the edge of the rug. There is enough room outside the sacred square for people to sit. Inside the square is the altar, the Yuwipi man, and all his medicine objects—the sacred peace pipe, which is never missing from a ceremony of any importance, a pot filled with fresh, clear water, and a kettle of dog meat. The floor is covered with sagebrush.

The sponsor and the guests arrive and sit down on the floor along the walls, outside the sacred square of tobacco-ties. Once the ceremony starts, nobody may step into the square. The men sit down on one side, the women on the other. Pictures, mirrors, and

This painting dating from 1832 shows the interior of a Mandan medicine lodge.

Even today, medicine men are still curing the sick in the old Indian way, with herbs and prayers.

everything else that could reflect light are covered with blankets. Those present are even asked to take off their wristwatches and eyeglasses. The door and all the windows are likewise covered with quilts. Everybody present receives a twig of sagebrush, which forms a link, or conductor, between each person and the spirits which are about to come. Sweet grass is burned as incense. Its aromatic fragrance fills the room and puts everybody in the right mood.

Two helpers now tie the Yuwipi man's arms and hands securely to his body. Even his fingers are tied, one to the other. He is next wrapped tightly, head and all, into a quilt, a so-called star blanket. Once more a rawhide rope is tied around him until he looks like an Egyptian mummy. Two men then carefully place him face down in the center of the square. At once all lights are extinguished. The room is totally and utterly dark, as black as black can be. A voice begins to chant, a drum to beat. Strange things begin to happen. A

(1) The participants in a Yuwipi ceremony sit on the floor outside the square of sacred tobacco knots with their backs resting against the walls.

(2) The hands of the medicine man are tied behind him.

(3) He then is wrapped in a star blanket like a mummy.

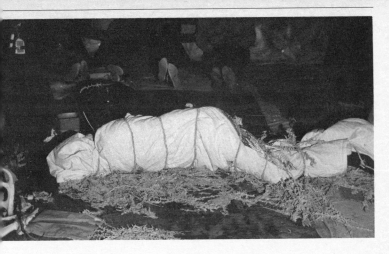

(4) Next, he is laid on the floor and all lights are extinguished. In total darkness the participants in the ceremony see little sparks of light flitting through the air and hear the voices of the spirits.

(5) When, at the end of the ceremony, the lamps are lit again, the medicine man sits untied and tells the listeners what the spirits have told him.

large bird seems to fly through the room. You can't see it, but you feel and hear the flapping of its huge wings. The house shakes as if gripped by a giant hand. The rattles jump from the floor and fly about the room, knock against the ceiling or your head. Little voices whisper in your ear.

Little sparks of light bounce off your shoulders or the walls. This tells you that the spirits are now present. And always there are the little voices, the chants, the drum. At last everything is quiet again. A kerosene lamp is lit. The Yuwipi man stands untied and unwrapped. He interprets what the spirits have told him. He explains about the cause of the disease, tells where to find a missing person, or announces who will win the next tribal election. All Sioux ceremonies have a happy ending. Everybody, in turn, has something good to say about the events of the night. The pipe goes from hand to hand, and finally comes a most important part of all Sioux rituals. Remember the twenty dollars worth of food? Somebody says in a loud voice: "Wa unyun tinkte!"—"Let us eat now!"

12 ▪ THE SUN DANCE

This year I want
to suffer more,
pierce my flesh
a little deeper,
dance harder,
so that there may be peace,
and the young men of our
tribe can come home.

PETE CATCHES, 1967
AT THE SUN DANCE

Each summer the religious life of the Plains Indians reached its high point in the sun dance. It was one of the outstanding features of their culture. In many tribes it was a rite of self-torture, where men pierced their breast muscles with skewers of wood and offered small pieces of their flesh to the Great Spirit. Even among the tribes which did not practice this form of self-torture, the sun dance was still a grueling ordeal. It meant dancing without food or water for four days, gazing at the sun, swaying back and forth, until the men fainted from exhaustion.

Preparations for the sun dance resembled the setting out of a war party. Scouts searched for a cottonwood tree worthy of the honor of becoming the sacred dance pole. Respectfully the leader addressed the tree: "I have chosen you. Be proud. I could have chosen another tree." Next a young warrior, who had distinguished himself by some brave deed in the months before the sun dance, was selected to count coup upon the tree. This was a great honor. Then four young maidens, chosen for their virtue, chopped down the tree. It was not allowed to fall to the ground but was caught by a group of men, who then carried it solemnly to the dance ground. As the procession came in sight, a throng of mounted warriors, upon a given signal, raced their horses to be the first to touch the sacred spot where the tree would stand. They jostled, wheeled, and wrestled, knocking each other off their ponies in their eagerness. The young brave who finally succeeded in counting the first coup upon the sacred spot was envied by all. His deed would bring him luck in battle.

The sacred sun dance circle, a ring of poles covered with leaves and branches, was then ready to receive the center pole. When the tree had finally been erected with all the proper ceremonies, the dance would begin. The self-torture usually took place on the fourth day. Men would pass thongs through the flesh of their backs and fasten buffalo skulls to them. They danced till the weight of the skulls ripped the thongs loose. Others hung from ropes attached to the top of the center pole and anchored in the flesh of their breasts. They danced until they had torn themselves free. Still others stood between four poles. From each pole rawhide thongs led to skewers in both their breasts and backs. These dancers had the hardest time to rip themselves loose. All this was endured, not to prove one's courage or endurance, but in obedience to a vow, to give thanks to the Great Spirit for help in battle or sickness. A dancer suffered by his own free will to help others and to show his selflessness.

For many years the sun dance was forbidden by the government. It was outlawed as barbaric and unchristian by people who did not understand it. During this time it could be performed only in secret. In 1936 the government relented. The white people admitted that forbidding the Indians to suffer for their faith had taken away their freedom of religion. Since then the dance has been held every year, proudly and in the open.

In 1967, the sun dance in Winner, South Dakota, was held as a peace offering and to protect from harm the many Sioux warriors

This picture, painted in 1832, shows that the sun dance was performed then as it is now. The dancer is undergoing a form of self-torture called "piercing," because the flesh of the dancer's chest is pierced with skewers. Rawhide thongs, attached to a pole, are fastened to the skewers. The dancer then pulls back until he has torn himself loose.

While most Plains tribes practiced the sun dance, some of them did it without piercing their flesh.

serving overseas. From the sacred cottonwood hung streamers of colored cloth offerings and bundles of tobacco. To its top was fastened a small image of a buffalo and a human figure. At the base of the center pole was a huge mandrake root resembling the body of a human being. On the last day of the dance, the four men who had vowed to have themselves pierced underwent purification in a sweat bath first. The dance ground was purified, too, with the incense of a braid of burning sweet grass. Four flags of colored calico marked out the sacred circle, a line which only the dancers were allowed to cross. A buffalo skull altar was set up. All dogs were

(1) A sun dance begins with the setting up of the center pole, the sacred cottonwood tree. Offerings to the Great Spirit are tied to the pole—long, streaming flags of colored cloth and many small tobacco bundles. Pine branches form a roof over a circle of poles, providing shade for the spectators. Shown here is a sun dance at Wounded Knee, in South Dakota.

THE SUN DANCE

(2) Dancers line up and pray at the beginning of the ceremony. One man carries the buffalo skull which will be a part of the sun dance altar.

(3) Each sun dancer wears wreaths of sage on his head and around his wrists. He carries his own medicine bundle on his breast. Throughout the whole dance he is blowing on a plumed whistle made of an eagle's wing bone. Women take part in the sun dance, but they do not pierce.

(6) At the end of the sun dance, the medicine man Pete Catches has broken free from the rawhide thong connecting him to the center pole. Pete Catches has eagle feathers fastened in the flesh of his arms and back. He has danced the sun dance many times.

(5) The Sioux medicine man Eagle Feathers has an eagle claw fastened in his flesh.

(4) At the end of the sun dance, which lasts for four days, the dancers who have made a special vow have themselves pierced. Blowing on their eaglebone whistles, they struggle painfully to tear themselves free.

chased away, which took some time, and then the dance began.

The procession was led by a young, beautiful girl carrying the peace pipe. She represented the holy buffalo woman who, in days long past, had brought the pipe to the Sioux people, instructed them in its use, and then changed herself into a white buffalo calf. The dancers wore wreaths of fragrant sage around their heads, and medicine bundles were dangling from their necks. The drum began to sound. After dancing and praying for a long time, the dancers went, one by one, to the altar. There they lay down, a piece of wood clenched between their teeth. A medicine man bit the flesh above their hearts until it was white and numb. Then he quickly and deftly pierced the skin with his knife. He inserted an eagle claw or a sagebrush stem in the wound and tied the end of a rawhide thong to it. The other end was fastened to the top of the sacred pole.

The medicine man then took the dancers by the hand and led them to their stations. He, himself, was one of the dancers and was pierced like the others. Eagle feathers were embedded in his flesh, and forty tiny pieces of skin, about a quarter of an inch square, had been cut from each of his arms as a sacrifice to the spirits.

Each dancer held a plumed eagle-bone whistle in his mouth. The shrill sound of the whistles mingled with the beating of the drum. The four men danced forward to the pole and back again until their skin was stretched to the breaking point. At last, with a great effort of will power, they broke free. The sun dance was over. The spectators lined up to thank and to shake the hands of the dancers who had suffered for them all. The big mandrake root was cut up and its many pieces distributed among those present. It was very good medicine for preventing many sicknesses. Once more a prayer was said, a prayer for peace and understanding among all men. Then everybody, including the white spectators, were invited to come and eat.

13 ▪ THE GHOST TRAIL

*Nothing lasts except the
earth and the mountains.*

DEATH SONG

Life and death for the Plains Indians were one never-ending circle. The sun died each day to be reborn again in the morning. Plants withered in the cold of winter to sprout again at the time of greening. So it was with the tribe. The spirits of the dead walked the ghost trail to the land of many lodges. Here stood the countless tepees of their forefathers. Here the prairie was always green, the sun shone, and the buffalo and antelope were without number.

The Indians did not bury their dead. They placed their remains upon a high scaffold where the spirits could escape into the winds and the clouds. Sometimes they were placed in the crotch of a tree or on a stone ledge. Men were laid to rest with their medicine bundles, shields, drums, and weapons; women with their sewing kits and awl cases. A braid of the dead person's hair was put into a bundle, where other braids from those gone long before were kept. Dead men's moccasins had their soles beaded in intricate patterns, unlike those of a living person. In these moccasins the departed spirits would find it easy to make the long journey to the land of the many lodges.

A favorite horse was sometimes slain, so that a warrior's spirit would not have to walk to the happy hunting grounds. The Indians explained it to the horse, saying: "Grandchild, your owner loved you. Now he is dead. He wants to take you with him on the spirit trail. Carry him safely. Go willingly!" The slain horse's head and tail were then tied to the funeral scaffold.

The dead person's relatives, men as well as women, cut off their

(*Left*) The Plains Indians did not bury their dead. They placed their remains upon a high scaffold where the spirits could escape into the winds and the clouds. Sometimes the dead were placed in the fork of a tree, or on a stone ledge.

(*Right*) At a warrior's death his favorite horse was slain, so that his spirit would not have to walk to the Happy Hunting Grounds. The horse was told: "Grandchild, your owner loved you. He wants to take you with him. Go willingly."

hair and painted themselves with mourning colors to show their grief. Sometimes they did not stop at this but wounded themselves to express their sorrow and sense of loss. Men pierced their flesh with sticks, some even cut off their little fingers. Women gashed their arms and legs with sharp flints or knives. One very old lady, recalling the customs of her childhood, said, "I don't know whether I wept more about my dead grandfather or about my cut legs."

In some tribes a chief or a famous warrior was laid to rest in his own tepee. His body would be propped against his willow-stick backrest, and he would be dressed in his best war shirt and plumes, with a well-filled pipe within arm's reach. A pony tail flying from a lodgepole told the passing rider that this was the grave of a great man. There it would remain until the wind, the weather, and time destroyed it.

Nobody would ever disturb a man's last resting place or take anything from it, even if he had been an enemy. The Santee have a story about this. A party of four warriors was out on a raid against the Assiniboin. They happened to come across the funeral tepee of

an enemy chief. They could guess who was buried inside by the deeds of war painted on the outside of the tepee. It was placed high on a hill and the four Santees rode down to the river to make their camp. Three of them were young men, the fourth was a wise, old warrior.

The young men were thinking aloud: "This was a great chief, he must have many fine and useful things in his tent. They are no good to him now, but we could use them. Besides, he was our enemy. The things with him are probably trophies taken from us in battle. We will only take what rightfully belongs to us anyhow."

"You are very badly brought up young men," said the old warrior. "What you propose to do is wrong. I will have nothing to do with this. Besides, the ghost of the dead chief will defend his things."

"We don't believe in ghosts," said the greedy young men.

While the three of them stealthily crept up the hill again, the old warrior quickly covered his body and face with white clay and mud that he had scooped up from the riverbank. Then he quickly raced up the hill, transformed into a horrid, fear-inspiring apparition. When the young men arrived on top, they found themselves confronted by a ghost. "Who dares to disturb my rest?" roared the pale figure, waving his arms and letting out a piercing shriek. The young men were stricken with fright and ran down the hill as fast as they could, but in their fear they stumbled all over the place. The pale ghost overtook them one by one, touching them as he did so. As they felt the touch of his cold, clammy fingers, the young men fainted with terror, one after the other. The old warrior was back at the campsite long before them. He had washed off the mud and was sitting by the warm fire when the young men returned, shivering and gloomy.

"The dead chief did not like us very much," they reported shamefacedly.

"I hope you learned something from all this," commented the old warrior, calmly smoking his pipe.

For the most part a dead person's possessions were given away, in times past as well as today.

Two other customs are still kept by Indians who believed in old ways. A little bit of food is put aside at every meal for the spirits of the dead. Even though it is only a small morsel, it will feed many departed ones.

Tattooing is another custom which has to do with a person's afterlife. Most Plains Indians still have little tattoo marks on their wrists or faces. Often these are just a few blue dots or a small design, perhaps a few letters. To the outsider these are meaningless. Many Indians believe that on their way to the spirit land they will come to a bridge which leads across a dark river. At the entrance to the bridge, they think, they will find the owl women, who will examine their wrists for tattoo marks. These serve as a kind of admission. If the owl women find a tattoo, they will let the bearer pass; if not, they will throw the untattooed one over the bridge into the river below.

Death, to the Indian, was as natural as birth. Man died to go to the spirit world. The tribe lived on. The younger ones took the place of the old ones. The Dakota have a legend that illustrates this. On a high mountaintop sits an old woman before her tepee. She is alone, except for her dog who never sleeps. She is decorating a large buffalo robe with beautiful designs of porcupine quills. If the designs were ever finished, hers would be the most splendid buffalo robe on earth.

Today Indians have to be buried in the white man's way, but they still have Indian symbols carved on their headstones and wooden markers.

A fire with a boiling kettle of food burns before the old woman. Every now and then she puts the buffalo robe down from her lap and gets up to stir the kettle. Whenever she does so, the dog who never sleeps pulls out the threads and quills, so that the old woman has to start all over again. If ever the dog should fail to do this and the robe should be finished, the world would come to an end. "There is wisdom in that story," said an old medicine man. "Our work should never be all finished. We must leave something to do for those coming after us. If we had done it all, if we left everything perfect, what would be the sense of living then? Then the world would really come to an end."

14 ▪ A RISING DEMAND FOR BEAVER HATS

*I have seen the irresistible
march of civilization and
beheld its sweeping desolation.
And I have held converse with
the happy thousands, living as yet
beyond its influence, who had not
been crushed, nor have yet
dreamed of its approach. . . .*

GEORGE CATLIN

White men in the 1800s wore the stovepipe hats we still admire in the old family portraits of the time. They were made of beaver fur —durable, waterproof, and fashionable.

There was only one place, however, where beaver still existed in large numbers—the Indian Territory of the Plains. And so the first of the mountain men and trappers came with their long Kentucky rifles, their "strike a light" of steel and flint, their twists of chewing tobacco, and their traps. Some came on horseback, some in flatboats.

They were an independent lot, ornery as grizzly bears. They could fight their weight in wild cats. Sometimes they fought the Indians, sometimes they fought each other. And often they involved the Indian tribes in their feuds. They sang:

> *"Oh, I'm wild and woolly*
> *And full of fleas,*
> *Ain't never been curried*
> *Below the knees."*

They were never sick. Their chief complaint was that the constant wading in icy beaver ponds and streams gave them stiff joints, or

At the beginning of the nineteenth century fashionable Europeans liked to wear hats made of beaver fur. No well-dressed person wanted to be without such a hat, but the only place where beaver were still plentiful was the American West. With the price of pelts steadily rising, more and more white trappers came to the Great Plains.

rheumatism, in their old age. But this was no great problem, as they seldom lived that long.

They had a great knack for surviving, though. One mountain man, the famous John Colter, was caught trapping in Blackfoot country. The Blackfoot Indians did not fancy white men coming into their territory and getting the beaver pelts that they themselves could trade for guns and blankets at the Hudson Bay Company fort. Colter knew this well, but it was hard to keep a mountain man out of a place where he wanted to hunt and trap.

The Indians caught Colter, stripped him naked, and took his weapons. "Is the white man a good runner?" asked the chief. "The white man is a poor runner," answered Colter. "Even women and children can outrun him." The chief pointed ahead and said, "Run for your life!" They let him get ahead one or two hundred yards, then with a great war whoop, a crowd of young warriors started after him with lances and tomahawks. The chase went on and on, mile after mile. Thorns and cactus tore at Colter's naked body. Blood gushed from his nostrils. His heart seemed to burst. At last he dared to look back. Only one huge brave had been able to keep up with him. As both runners gained their second wind, the race went on at an even faster pace.

At last Colter could run no more. Reeling and stumbling, he turned to face his pursuer. The Indian lunged at Colter with his spear. The trapper caught it and broke off the stone blade, which he plunged like a dagger into the Blackfoot's chest.

Distant yells reminded him that the rest of his pursuers were not far behind. On the open prairie he had no chance to hide, but far ahead he saw clumps of trees along a riverbank. When he finally reached them and plunged into the willows, he was, for a few precious minutes, out of sight. He saw a beaver dam rising above the water. He dove into the icy stream to find the underwater entrance. If it were too narrow, he would be trapped and would drown.

He squeezed through the entrance and felt something glide along his legs. It was the beaver, in a great hurry to get out. The top of the dam, with the chamber that constituted the beaver's living quarters, was above the water. In this small space, he could breathe. He stayed there in the icy darkness for two nights. When he finally struggled out of his strange place of refuge, the Blackfoot warriors had long given up searching for him.

He was naked, unarmed, and three hundred miles from the nearest trading post. He traveled day and night without sleep, his skin in shreds, living off roots and the bark of trees. But he reached the fort and survived. The place where this happened is now called Yellowstone National Park, but it was first known as Colter's Hell.

The Indians understood the mountain men, even though they often had to fight them. The mountain men led a similar life and were as wild and free as the Indians. They lived by the same code. They left nature as they found it. Often they took an Indian wife and joined her tribe. Once they tasted the freedom of the Plains, the

The early trappers and mountain men were an independent lot. They wanted to live as far away from civilization as they possibly could. They wore long hair, shaggy beards, slouch hats, and fringed buckskin shirts embroidered with beads. They dressed and lived like Indians and often married Indian women.

stillness of the mountains, they were reluctant to return to civilization. One of them expressed their feelings when he wrote: "Darn the white diggins while thar's buffler in the hills." By 1840 the beavers were trapped out. Somebody discovered how to make hats out of felt, and the mountain men disappeared.

But the traders stayed. The Indians still had plenty of valuable buffalo robes, elk skins, and other furs to swap for the white man's powder, lead, tobacco, muskets, coffee, knives, awls, blankets, bells, and beads. To protect their goods, the traders built stockades and blockhouses, Fort Union, Fort Laramie, Bent's Fort.

The white man's things, which the traders carried, changed the Indians' lives. Iron-tipped weapons replaced stone arrowheads. Men quickly forgot how to make a fire with drilling stick and bowstring, once they had the "strike a light." It was easier to cook in a kettle than in a buffalo-stomach pouch, and beading was better than wearing down one's teeth by chewing on porcupine quills to make them flat and soft. And oh, how good it was to drink hot, sweet coffee from a tin cup!

Coffee was not the only new drink the traders introduced. Many of their things made life easier for the Indians, but whiskey did not. The law forbade giving it to the Indians, but it was a cheap and profitable merchandise. Besides, the law was far away. A trader could get a fine buffalo robe for just two glasses of "white lightning." Indians were not used to whiskey. A few swallows made them drunk. A chief said, "The white men taught us so much, why didn't they teach us how to drink?"

Traders diluted the whiskey until it was mostly Missouri water. They added pepper, gunpowder, and tobacco to give it a "kick" and to fool their customers. It still had enough bite to make an Indian drunk, so that he brawled and forgot how a warrior should behave.

The traders built stockades and forts surrounded with palisades from which they carried on their fur trade.

White traders brought the Indians many useful things—iron pots, sewing needles, steel knives, and pretty glass beads. But they also brought with them whisky and the smallpox which wiped out whole tribes.

It made some Indians into loafers and beggars who hung about the fort, ready to do anything for a drop of whiskey.

But the deadliest items the traders brought with them were the white man's diseases—smallpox, tuberculosis, measles, and cholera. The Indians' bodies had no built-in resistance against these new and unknown illnesses. Consequently, the tribes most friendly to the whites, and in closest contact with the traders, suffered most. The Pawnee and Catlin's beloved Mandan were the hardest hit.

After the smallpox epidemic of 1837, only 23 Mandan men, 40 women, and 65 children were left out of 1,800 people! The prairies were strewn with abandoned villages, empty tepees, and decaying bodies. The survivors did not have strength enough to hunt or to bury their dead. Despairing of the future, many survivors committed suicide. Death stalked the prairies as the golden age of the Plains drew to an end.

The more isolated, roving tribes were spared for a time, though the vile, horrible new diseases spread as far as the Blackfoot country. After the first wave of epidemics had run its course, the Indians' spirit revived. The prairies still teemed with buffalo. If the Great Spirit would take pity on his red children, all might yet be well. But new, vast, and uncontrollable forces were already at work, forces which would not merely kill, as the smallpox did, but which would forever end the proud, free life on the rolling prairie. The Indians had met the trapper and the trader. They were now about to meet another type of white man, one who would not be satisfied with riches gained from the fur trade. This newcomer did not want pelts or beautifully decorated buffalo robes. He wanted the red man's land —and the vast plains were not big enough to hold both the new settlers and the Indians.

15 ▪ THE COVERED WAGONS

*They told us they only
wanted a little land,
as much as a wagon would
take between the wheels.
You can see now what
it was they wanted.*

BLACK ELK SPEAKS

In 1830, a New York farmer founded a new religion and would soon get into trouble with his neighbors. In 1848, a man digging a ditch in faraway California found a small, glittering lump of yellow metal. A politician and speculator created a land boom in order to make money; a newspaper man wrote a fanciful story. Like a pebble that gains momentum and grows into a mighty avalanche sweeping everything before it, these incidents set in motion forces that were to engulf the Plains.

Three things were to drive the Plains Indians from their hunting grounds on to the reservations: gold hunger, land hunger, and the hunger for news. Each newspaper story announcing a gold strike in Colorado or Montana or the opening of a new territory to homesteaders had a magic influence on the multitudes in the bursting, overcrowded cities of the East. Writers of the time speak of "Land Fever" and "Gold Fever," and these were good words to describe the strange madness which seemed to spread through the towns and villages.

Artisans displaced by the machines of the new industrial age, farmers whose land had become barren from too many harvests, immigrants fleeing from the tyranny of European governments, men running away from creditors and responsibilities, all joined the

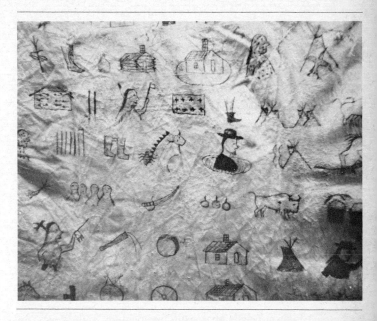

Plains Indians did not write down their history, but in some tribes men kept wintercounts—buffalo skins on which each year was depicted by the drawing of some event which had occurred during its twelve months. The wintercount shown here tells us much about the white man's conquest of the Plains. The top row shows two houses put up by settlers on Indian land. Next to the houses we see the figure of an Indian covered with red spots—this was during the year in which "Many People Died of Smallpox." In the middle row, the picture of a man with a beard, a black hat, and a black robe symbolizes the year in which the first white priest arrived. The saber in the row below means a year in which the "Long Knives"—the U. S. cavalry—attacked. The last two rows show more white homes being built and more missionaries arriving.

ever-growing stream of humanity that was once again rolling westward across the wide Missouri.

They were spurred on by a dream of empire, by catchwords such as "Go West, Young Man" or "Manifest Destiny." They harbored dreams of a Golden West, where each of them would carve out his his own, personal empire with a spade, a pickax, or a rusty pan.

Gold hunger brought many white men to the Plains. Mining towns sprang up overnight wherever gold or silver was found.

These towns were deserted as soon as the gold gave out. Ghost towns became the abodes of wolves and coyotes. The goldseekers left nothing behind but ruins, trash, and mine dumps. Pollution is no new problem on the Plains.

These were the simple-minded ones. With them came men, much fewer in number, who would put up a saloon somewhere along the way, or a gambling place, or start a stage coach line. They were the future governors, mayors, judges, and hardware store owners. They had few dreams, but they would wind up with most of the gold.

There were four distinct "invasions" of the Plains between 1840 and the Civil War. The first, brought on by the successful war with Mexico, was made up of people streaming into the rich, newly conquered territories of New Mexico, Arizona, and California. Among them were the future cattle barons. They moved along the Santa Fe Trail.

The second invasion was carried out by settlers bound for Oregon—a land of milk and honey with the richest soil in the world, if one were to believe the glowing descriptions of the land speculators and companies which tried to attract settlers. They moved westward along the Oregon Trail, starting in huge caravans out of Independence, Missouri.

The third wave was made up of the forty-niners, named after the big gold rush of that year. They were California-bound fortune seekers who followed the Oregon Trail as far as Fort Bridger, and then made their way through the mountain passes to the California gold fields. When gold was found in Colorado and Montana, part of this stream of humanity was diverted to these regions, following the Platte River into Colorado, or up to the northern gold fields by way of the Bozeman Trail.

The fourth and last were the Mormons, led by Brigham Young, bent on building the New Zion in the wilderness. The strange fact was that all these people, with the exception of the Mormons, did not intend to settle in the Plains which was, as you remember, "fit only for wolves, bears, and uncivilized savages." The Mormons, in fact, occupied no more than the southern fringe of the Plains and played only a comparatively minor role in the Indian wars that were to follow.

If the gold seekers and the settlers bound for Oregon could have reached their destination any way other than across Indian Territory, they gladly would have done so. But the only alternative to reach Oregon or California was to go by ship around Cape Horn. Such a trip was just as difficult and dangerous as the overland route, and it took longer and cost more. And so the multitudes kept coming through the Plains.

"Look here," said the travelers to the Indians whose land they crossed, "we are just moving through, we are not staying. All we want is the right of way. We'll even pay you for letting us cross. A lame cow, a blanket, a bottle of whiskey. The land is so big and we'll only make these two ruts through it, just as wide as a wagon." The Indians found out, to their dismay, that it was not such a simple matter. These newcomers were different from the lean mountain men, who had carried all their possessions in a blanket roll slung across their shoulders. There were so incredibly many of the newcomers, for one thing, and they did not travel light. They came in huge, ox-drawn, covered wagons called prairie schooners, which was not a bad name for a vehicle in which to cross the "Sea of Grass."

Along their path they littered the prairie with their trash and discarded, broken-down things, a forewarning of what civilization would bring to the Plains. They hunted for meat along their route, and what game they didn't shoot, they scared away. Their trails divided the buffalo herds, which would stay on one side or the other.

And so the natural migration and wanderings of the Indians'

The settlers came in covered wagons called "Prairie Schooners"—not a bad name for a vehicle which had to cross the famous Sea of Grass.

living food reserve was interrupted. Some tribes found it suddenly difficult to find the buffalo in their accustomed places. The settlers carried their families with them in their prairie schooners, along with everything necessary to settle down. What would prevent them from building a sod house and starting a farm if they saw a piece of land which suited them? And what would prevent the miners from looking for gold in places nearer and more convenient than distant California? The Indians were afraid of the many white men. The white men were afraid of the Indians. Neither side trusted the other, and the government sent in the U.S. Cavalry to protect them all and keep the peace—at least this was supposedly the reason. The situation was, as one trader said, "full of tinder, only waiting for a spark to set it aflame."

16 ▪ THE MORMON'S COW

Greed and avarice
on the part of the whites—
in other words the almighty dollar—
is at the bottom of nine-tenths
of all our Indian troubles.

GENERAL GEORGE CROOK

From 1850 on, the history of the Plains developed into an endless repetition of broken treaties and promises. Its pages were written in blood and tears. As soon as the settlers and miners took over a certain region, the Indians upon whose lands they had trespassed were called together to make a treaty. They were then cajoled and threatened into giving up part of their hunting grounds. They had more land than they needed, they were told. They must sell some of their land.

The commissioners who dealt with the Indians distributed thousands of dollars worth of trade goods as bribes. Some chiefs were taken to Washington to see the "Great White Father" and to be impressed with the irresistible power of the white man. They were wined and dined and given stovepipe hats and ridiculous frock coats with golden epaulets to make them more pliable to the commissioners' demands. Chief was set against chief, and tribe against tribe. The demoralized bands of loafers, who hung around the forts in hope of handouts and whiskey, were induced to sign away lands which did not belong to them.

Many fair and flowery promises were made to get the chiefs to "touch the pen" and make their marks on documents which they could neither read nor understand. Each time, they were told that *this* particular treaty would end all their troubles forever. If they

The history of the Plains is a history of broken treaties. Agreements with Indians were broken before the ink on the paper was dry.

would just sign once more, all the rest of the vast plains would be theirs, "as long as the grass shall grow, as long as the sun shall shine, in perpetuity, forever and ever, in all eternity." Just touch the pen and the army would protect them against further encroachment by white immigrants. And they would get many presents, $5,000 worth, $50,000 worth, $500,000 worth. For ten years, for fifty years, for a hundred years. Just sign, sign, sign!

These treaties, which were supposed to last as long as the sun and moon shone upon the plains, were usually broken before the ink was dry. Often Congress arbitrarily cut the price for which the Indians had sold their land to a half or even a tenth of the sum agreed upon in the document. Much of the goods was stolen before reaching the tribes, and the army made no effort to keep the settlers out of the shrinking Indian Territory.

A string of forts had been built to protect the overland routes and the wagon trains from the "bloodthirsty red miscreants." These forts were garrisoned by the "Long Knives," as the Indians called the cavalry troopers with their heavy sabers, and the "Walk-a-heaps" with their "wagon guns"—infantry soldiers with their cannon. The soldiers were a mixed lot. Among them were many "snow birds," men who enlisted in the fall for the sake of warm and cozy winter quarters and who went over the hill to fresh territory as soon as the snows had melted. They were bounty jumpers whose motto was "Get your enlistment money now, desert later."

By and large, however, the troopers were a hard-riding, hard-drinking, and hard-fighting lot. The officers thirsted for action and glory at any price. The American peacetime army was small. At times its strength was reduced to as few as twenty thousand men. Officer's pay was low, available commands few, and advancement slow. Men became white-haired before attaining the rank of captain or major. There was an intense competition among junior officers, and the only way to promotion was a successful battle against the Indians. The temptation to stir things up, rather than to keep the peace, was very strong.

A modern photograph taken at Fort Laramie shows the old junior officer's quarter. A sudden call to arms has interrupted a poker game, leaving the playing cards and half-filled whisky glasses still on the table. Garrison life in the West was hard and, except for occasional Indian raids, dull. Entertainments were few. Many lonely young officers sought distraction in gaming and drinking.

A longhorn cow, like this one shown surrounded by her wild relatives, started the Indian wars of 1854.

The treaties contained many clauses about compensation for damages done by Indians to whites, and by whites to Indians. But the Indians could not read them, and besides, they did not understand the white man's strange ideas about property. They were mystified by his frantic digging for the yellow metal, and it angered them when settlers declared that they owned a parcel of land and fenced it in. Even a child knew that the Great Spirit had created the Plains for all people. A tribe would consider a certain vast region as its hunting ground, but as for a single person claiming to own a certain piece of land, that was just plain foolishness. Land belonged to no one and to everyone at the same time.

As far as the western plains are concerned, the beginning of the Indian wars is generally considered to be 1854. In that year a small band of Sioux Indians came upon a sick cow that had been abandoned by a Mormon settler. The Indians had not found any buffalo and were hungry. They slaughtered the cow and ate it.

Somehow the Mormon found out. He also knew about the Treaty of Fort Laramie, made with a number of western tribes in 1851. By this treaty the Indians opened the "Holy Road," up the Platte River and through the western mountains, to the white settlers in return for $5,000 per year for a period of fifty years. The Indians, of course, got only a small fraction of the goods promised them.

The thrifty Mormon saw a chance to turn a quick penny. He went to Fort Laramie and demanded twenty-five dollars for his beast. Among the fort's officers was Lieutenant John L. Grattan, who prevailed upon his commandant to let him handle the matter and bring in the offenders. Grattan was a fire-eater who told everybody who would listen that with ten men at his back he could defeat the whole Cheyenne nation, and with twenty men all the Indians of the Plains.

Grattan took thirty men and two howitzers into the Indian camp circle and demanded money as well as the surrender of the culprits. The lieutenant was drunk. So was his interpreter. Grattan had told his men he "hoped to God there would be a fight." He was about to have his wish granted.

The Indians were puzzled. They had no money. They didn't even know what money was. They offered ponies in exchange for the famous cow and proposed to talk things over with the agent at the fort. This was not what Grattan wanted. He loaded his cannon with grapeshot and opened fire, killing a number of Indians, among them two chiefs. The Sioux counter attacked, and in a short time Grattan and everyone in his command was dead. This was the famous Grattan Massacre. It took place on the 19th of August, 1854, and from this moment on, war would rage on the Plains until the last Indian surrendered.

Reading the history of the Indian wars depended on one's outlook. It is easy to tell who had been the winner of a particular struggle. If the Indians won, it was usually called a massacre—if the army won, it was called a battle. Thus we speak of the Battle of the Washita or the Battle of Wounded Knee, even though the dead were mostly Indian women and children. On the other hand we have the Grattan Massacre, and the Fetterman Massacre, fights in which the slain were all professional soldiers with modern arms. But as attitudes have changed, these two terms are often used interchangeably.

Another oddity of western history is the tale of the unspeakable

The confrontation between Lieutenant Grattan and the Cheyennes must have looked very much like this drawing which dates from the same time.

tortures practiced as a matter of course by the "red fiends" upon all victims unlucky enough to fall into their hands. "Always save the last bullet for yourself" was the advice given to new recruits as they arrived at the western outposts. The warfare of the Plains was cruel enough, and a wounded enemy had little chance of having his life spared. But systematic torture at the stake, such as practiced by the Iroquois in the eighteenth century, was unknown among the western tribes. Some of the worst atrocities of the Indian wars were committed by white soldiers, especially by volunteer regiments of undisciplined and lawless cowhands and homesteaders. White troopers took scalps just as the Indians did, with one important difference. Whites were often paid a bounty, ten dollars for a scalp of an Indian brave, five dollars for the scalp of a woman or child. The Grattan Massacre was followed by a punitive expedition under General William L. Harney. His mission was to teach the Sioux that it was wrong to fight back when they were fired upon by cannons. Harney surprised a village which considered itself at peace, killed over eighty Indians, and brought some seventy captive women and children back in a triumphal parade.

The Civil War brought these "Indian troubles" to a temporary halt. The white men had their hands full fighting each other. For a while the settlers stopped coming, the guns grew silent, and the war whoops subsided as a deceptive peace settled in the Plains.

During some fights, white soldiers deliberately killed Indian women and children. Attacking an Indian village at Sand Creek, Colonel Chivington, a former minister of a Christian church, told his soldiers: "Kill 'em all, big and small, nits make lice!" By this he meant that it was smart to kill small Indian boys before they grew up to become warriors who would shoot back. Today some Indians say, "Sand Creek was our My Lai."

17 ▪ NITS MAKE LICE

Kill and scalp all,
big and small,
nits make lice!

COLONEL JOHN M. CHIVINGTON

The years following the Civil War constitute a very dark chapter in history. Americans shudder when they hear of Hitler's concentration camps and the murder of millions of Jews. The twentieth century coined a word for these crimes—*genocide,* which means the extermination of a whole people. It is a sad fact that in the isolated, faraway plains, genocide was practiced against the Indians. In the opinion of many soldiers and settlers, the only good Indian was a dead Indian. Some men even went so far as to issue to the tribes blankets that came from the beds of cholera and smallpox patients —the earliest attempt at germ warfare.

It was the era of the "Nits make Lice" policy, which simply meant that it was good policy to kill Indian women before they could give birth to sons, and to kill boys before they grew up into warriors who could fight back. It is only fair to say that these advocates of murder were opposed by good and fair-minded people, both in Washington and in the West, men who tried their best to protect the Indians from the worst injustices. Unfortunately, they were seldom in the right place at the right time and were thus unable to influence events.

In 1864, when some usual skirmishes took place between Indians and the miners who had ventured too far into the hunting grounds, the Indian haters saw their chance. They exhibited the bodies of a murdered settler's family in Denver and whipped up feeling for another big expedition to punish the "savages." The leader was

Colonel John M. Chivington, a former clergyman. He had with him about seven hundred volunteer militiamen, mostly miners, gamblers, cowpunchers, and saloon keepers.

Chivington set out determined to find some Indians to kill. He was told of an Indian camp at Sand Creek, not far from Fort Lyon. The chief of the Indian camp was Black Kettle of the Southern Cheyenne. He was a man of peace. Again and again he had told his people not to resist the white men. It would be suicide. There were too many of them. He had made friends with the commandant at Fort Lyon. He had pitched his camp at Sand Creek with the permission of that officer. The army would protect him and his people, so he had been told. Above his camp waved a large American flag. The Stars and Stripes was a powerful medicine, Black Kettle had explained to his people. It would shield the Cheyenne from any harm.

But the flag did not help them when Chivington surrounded Black Kettle's village on all sides and poured a murderous fire into it. After the first shock, the badly outnumbered warriors defended themselves bravely, bows and arrows against Chivington's artillery. Major Anthony, one of the combatants, reported: "I never saw more bravery displayed by any set of people on the face of the earth than by these Indians. They would charge us singlehanded, determined to kill someone before being killed themselves."

When it was pointed out to Chivington that the village was full of women and children, and he was asked what to do with them, he uttered his famous words: "Kill them all, big and small, nits make lice!" Over five hundred Cheyennes were slain, and only a small number of them were warriors of fighting age. Babies had their brains dashed out by the soldiers. Robert Bent, the son of the famous trader, was an eyewitness. He described how the helpless people were hacked to pieces. The soldiers mutilated and scalped the dead "such as

Between 1854 and 1879, warfare between whites and Indians never ceased. In most cases the white intruder was the aggressor.

With mounting anger the Indian watched the campfires of the soldiers who were building roads across his hunting grounds, in defiance of all treaties.

no Indian ever did." The final scenes of the movie *Soldier Blue* show what happened at Sand Creek with horrifying realism. It was one of the few times Hollywood depicted history as it really happened and not as a romantic, prettified adventure story in which the dashing cavalrymen are always the "good guys."

A few surviving Cheyenne children were exhibited in the Denver Opry House, like so many circus freaks, together with the scalps of their parents. The Denver News ran a headline: "Colorado Soldiers Have Again Covered Themselves With Glory." But there was a public outcry as the real facts of the Sand Creek Massacre became known. Kit Carson, a rough and tough frontiersman not known for his sentimentality, described Chivington's deed as the "action of a coward and a dog." An inquiry was ordered and rather than face up to it, Chivington resigned. Unfortunately, this did not bring the Cheyenne women and children back to life.

The survivors of the Sand Creek Massacre fled north to the Powder River country, to their friends the Northern Cheyenne, Sioux, and Arapaho. They told the story of what had happened to them and they passed the war pipe. Whoever smoked it pledged himself to fight to the death. No one refused it. Among those who took the solemn four puffs were some of the greatest fighting leaders of the Plains: Red Cloud, Sitting Bull, Roman Nose, Crazy Horse.

The soldiers, too, were led by men who had become famous during the Civil War and whose names were known to every American: Sherman, Sheridan, Crook, Terry, Miles, Custer.

The next round of battles was, as usual, opened with a big peace conference at Fort Laramie in 1865–66. The Indians were now offered the Powder River country, the Dakotas, and much of Montana and Wyoming. The commissioners hid from them the fact that the treaty gave the government the right to build a road through this region and to maintain a number of forts along it.

The situation was once summed up perfectly by one of the white commissioners: "If the lands of a white man are taken, civilization brands him as a coward and a slave if he submits to the wrong. Here civilization made its contract and guaranteed the rights of the weaker party. The treaty was broken, but not by the savage. If the Indian resists, civilization, with the ten commandments in one hand and the sword in the other, demands his immediate extermination. These Indians saw their former homes overrun by a greedy population, thirsting for gold. They saw their game driven away, they must go."

While the peace talks were going on, the army was already moving into the Powder River country, building forts and widening trails. When Red Cloud heard about this, he walked out of the conference, followed by the other chiefs. They knew what a road through their country would mean.

The famous Chief Red Cloud, of the Oglala Sioux, defeated the army's attempt to build the Bozeman Road and for a few years stemmed the tide of white settlers and miners.

The road in question was the Bozeman Trail leading to the gold fields in Montana. The Indians called it, with good reason, the Thieves' Road. The man in charge of fortifying the Bozeman Trail was Colonel Henry Carrington. He named his chief stockade Fort Phil Kearney after a Civil War general. He soon found himself besieged in his fort by the whole might of the Sioux and Cheyenne. They kept up a guerilla warfare around the fort that made further operations by the troops impossible.

As winter came, it became necessary for Carrington to send out daily wood-cutting parties to keep his fort warm. These were often harassed by the Indians. On December 21, 1866, the company of wood cutters was attacked in force. Lookouts reported this to Carrington, who quickly organized a relief force. The command of this rescue party was given to Captain William Judd Fetterman, a hothead who had said: "Give me eighty men and I'll ride through the whole Sioux Nation!" This was considerably more than the twenty men which Grattan had thought sufficient to defeat all Plains Indians.

It so happened that Fetterman had exactly eighty men in his relief force, among them an officer who had been transferred East, but who did not want to go before he had taken an Indian scalp. Fetterman had strict orders only to make his way to the wood cutters and to bring them safely back to the stockade. Under no circumstances was he to pursue the Indians or venture beyond a certain ridge. But a group of warriors challenging him to a fight, and calling the soldiers cowards and women, proved too much for him. He ordered a charge right over the fateful ridge he was not supposed to cross.

The attack on the wood-cutting party had only been a feint to draw the cavalry out. Fetterman ran into an ambush by hundreds of warriors led by Crazy Horse and Red Cloud, and his command was wiped out to the last man. The captain saved the last bullet for for himself. He had accomplished one thing: He proved that eighty men were not enough to "ride through the whole Sioux Nation." This fight is known as the Fetterman Massacre, and it forced the army to abandon its line of forts and to give up the Bozeman Trail.

While the Indians had successfully defended their northern hunting grounds, they were losing in Colorado. There Major George A. Forsyth, who had risen from private soldier to general during the Civil War, had formed a special command of Indian fighters. They were frontiersmen and scouts who would make war Indian style, by raids and ambushes, employing only small forces. Forsyth had about fifty men, who were well armed with Colts and the latest repeating rifles.

At Fort Phil Kearney, the Sioux and Cheyenne under Red Cloud and Crazy Horse wiped out Captain Fetterman's command of eighty men and forced the abandonment of the fort.

On September 17, 1868, on a little sand pit in the middle of the Arikaree River of eastern Colorado, Forsyth got into a fight with a band of Northern Cheyenne led by the famous Chief Roman Nose. This chief was a giant, six feet four inches tall, with a hawklike profile from which he derived his name. His feats of bravery were legendary. Roman Nose owned a handsome war bonnet which was believed to make him bulletproof. The chief watched the battle from afar, instead of fighting in the thick of it as was his habit. The Indians missed their indomitable chief. Why did he not come to lead them?

The chief told them that he had unwittingly eaten food handled with an iron fork. This was very bad medicine, because he was bulletproof only as long as he kept a taboo that forbade him to eat anything touched by iron. "If I fight today," said Roman Nose, "I shall be killed."

But as the battle grew desperate and his friends fell, the chief calmly put on his war bonnet and led a do-or-die charge. He received a fatal wound and died, as he himself had predicted. Forsyth was wounded and Lieutenant Frederick H. Beecher, his second in command, killed. To honor him, this grim battle has been called the Beecher Island Fight.

Much has been said in this chapter about forts and army posts which had been built to hem the Indians in and to advance the white man's frontier. Some of these old forts have survived the years of abandonment and neglect to become museums where the modern tourist can obtain a glimpse of the colorful past.

At Fort Robinson, Nebraska, for example, the visitor can see a reconstructed trader's shop, or he can walk across the parade ground to the prison site where the great warrior Crazy Horse was killed.

At Fort Laramie, Wyoming, one can inspect the junior officers' living quarters or enter the cottages of their married seniors. Here, the visitor can admire the quaint lithographs on the walls, the buffalo rug on the floor, the bedspread made of a huge, black bearskin, and under the bed, the chamberpot with its delicate pattern of roses and forget-me-nots. In the officers' den, the grimy playing cards and half-filled whiskey glasses are still on the table, and the big brass spittoon is still waiting underneath it for a discarded cheroot or a wad of chewing tobacco. One expects that at any moment a group of officers in blue frockcoats will return to continue their interrupted card game. It all smacks of quaintness and the good old days. It seems like ancient history now.

The Indians' troubles with the U.S. Army are not altogether over. These days it is often the Army Corps of Engineers who is the enemy.

The corps likes to propose sites for hydroelectric dams. Some of these sites are on Indian reservations. Nowadays, treaties between the government and the Indians are supposed to be kept. The days of cheating the Indians of their rights are supposedly over. But this is not true where dams are concerned, even though the violated treaty had been signed by George Washington himself. The Seneca found this out when the Kinzua Dam was built on their reservation in Pennsylvania. Dams take precedence over treaties—and parts, or all, of a reservation can be condemned "in the public interest." In the Plains large parts of the Fort Belknap Reservation were flooded when the engineers harnessed the waters of the Missouri River to build the Garrison Dam.

Nor are dams the only problem. During World War II, the air force took over a large tract of the Pine Ridge Reservation in South Dakota for a bombing range. The Sioux Indians who live there were promised that the land would be returned. The day when this promise came due is long past. Sheep Mountain, which is part of the area taken, is now slated to become part of the Badlands National Monument. All during 1970, the Sioux of Pine Ridge demonstrated to get the bombing range back. A group of them occupied Sheep Mountain as a symbolic gesture. Even today, as this book is being written, Indians are fighting for their land.

18 ▪ THE COMING OF LONG HAIR

My every thought was ambitious—
not to be wealthy,
not to be learned,
but to be great
to future generations.

GEORGE ARMSTRONG CUSTER

The fights of Fetterman, Forsyth, Harney, and others had merely prepared the stage for a main actor who had long planned for himself a major role in the great drama of the Plains. One of the strangest and most controversial characters ever to appear in the West now arrived on the scene.

George Armstrong Custer was known as the Boy General, having attained that rank in his early twenties. It is hard to see what had made him a general, except his personal courage and his willingness to fight at all odds. Perhaps it was his celebrated Custer's Luck which had become proverbial throughout the army. His only tactics were head-on cavalry charges at full gallop with blaring trumpets and fluttering banners.

Custer was a stern disciplinarian and a stickler for military spit and polish. He himself wore fantastic, self-designed uniforms. As one writer described him: "His broad sombrero turned up, his golden locks dangling to his shoulders, the ends of his crimson cravat flying about him, gold galore spangling his jacket sleeves, a pistol in his boot and a ponderous claymore swaying at his side, a fringed buck-skin coat around his spare frame, so rode the wild daredevil with his pack of 30 dogs braying at his heels."

He deserted his command whenever he felt like visiting his wife.

He was frequently absent without leave, but he once ordered men who had run away from his regiment to be shot down on sight. He had an iron constitution, could outride and outlast any man in the regiment, and was annoyed when others could not keep up with him. Some of his men loved him, but most of them hated him intensely. To the Indians he was known as Long Hair.

Custer had worn the stars of a major general and commanded great masses of men. It had been sweet to hold that much power. In the peacetime army he had been reduced to the rank of a mere lieu-

George Armstrong Custer, known as the "Glory Hunter" and the "Boy General," was celebrated for his luck in battle—the famous "Custer's Luck."

A writer described Custer: "His broad sombrero turned up, his golden locks dangling to his shoulders, the ends of his crimson cravat flying about him, gold galore spangling his jacket sleeves, a pistol in his boot, and a ponderous claymore swaying at his side, a fringed buckskin coat around his spare frame, so rode the wild daredevil with his pack of thirty dogs braying at his heels."

tenant colonel, to the command of a single regiment. Even this regiment was not his, strictly speaking. He commanded it only while its colonel was on a prolonged recruiting drive. Custer yearned to be a general once more. The only way to attain that rank again, to win new glory and new headlines, was to fight Indians.

So here he was, in the cold November days of 1868, leading the famous crack regiment, the Seventh Cavalry, on a punitive expedition against the Indians, who did not expect an attack in wintertime. The plains were already covered with two feet of snow. Once again, the victims turned out to be Black Kettle and his village of Southern Cheyenne. He was still flying the American flag, still confident that his innocence and peaceful intentions would protect him. This is hard to understand, except that after the Sand Creek Massacre, he had been told that it was all a ghastly mistake, the work of a madman, that such a tragedy could never happen again. Surely, there could not be another man as crazy and cruel as Chivington had been.

Black Kettle wanted peace, but Custer wanted a battle at any price. The Cheyenne village was conveniently at hand. The fact that the Indians were sleeping peacefully was just one more example of Custer's Luck. The Indians Custer wanted to attack were holed up in a canyon behind Black Kettle's village. Custer could have found them if he had wanted to make the effort. Hostiles or friendlies, what did it matter, as long as he had his victory to keep him before the public eye.

For Black Kettle, the American flag became his winding sheet. He and his wife were killed by the first volley. His fourteen-year-old son was shot down trying to avenge his father. This Battle of the Washita was another Sand Creek Massacre, and once again, women and children were the chief victims. Also wiped out was a small detachment of troopers under Major Joel Elliott, who had been ordered to take the Indians in the flank. Custer seemed to have forgotten all about them in the heat of battle and made no move to rescue them, when there still might have been time. He did not even look for their bodies after the fight.

After the "battle" was over, the village was plundered and everything that could not be carried away was destroyed. The Indians' tepees, their warm winter robes, their stores of meat all went up in smoke, while the few survivors huddled half-naked in icy caves, with the prospect before them of either starving or freezing to death. Custer also ordered the camp's eight hundred ponies killed. He had no use for them, and he did not want the Indians to have them.

Captain Frederick W. Benteen, one of Custer's officers, described the scene: "That which cannot be taken away must be destroyed. Our chief exhibits his sharp-shooting and terrifies the crowd of frightened, captured squaws and papooses by dropping the struggling ponies in death near them. Ah! he is a clever marksman. Not even do the poor dogs escape his eye and aim as they drop dead or limp howling away. Now commences the slaughter of the ponies. Volley upon volley is poured into them by too hasty men, and they, limping, get away only to meet death from surer hands. The work progresses! The plunder having been culled over, is hastily piled, the wigwams thrown on it, and soon the whole is one blazing mass. And thus the glorious deeds of valor are celebrated. Take care! Do not trample on the dead bodies of that woman and child over there, as the brave band of the Seventh Cavalry strikes up the merry air, 'Ain't I glad to get out of the wilderness!'" The Battle of the Washita gave Custer the headlines he wanted, but Benteen's scornful report also found its way into the newspapers. Custer never forgave him for this.

In 1873 Custer led an expedition into the Black Hills of South Dakota These were the sacred grounds of the Sioux, which had been guaranteed to them by treaty for all eternity. Nearby was Bear Butte, the Cheyenne's most holy place. Custer reported "Gold in the Grassroots." This joyous message spread like wildfire, and the rush was on. Ugly mining towns, such as Deadwood, sprang up over night, and slag heaps, smelting furnaces, saloons, and gambling dens filled the valleys where the Sioux had once come to pray.

The army, at first, had made a half-hearted attempt to keep the gold seekers out, ignoring the fact that one of its own officers was responsible for their coming. But it soon gave up. It was useless to try and stem the tide. Government policy had changed anyway. Nobody pretended any more that the treaties would, or should, be kept. The free and glorious life of the Plains Indians was finally

Custer and the army employed Crows, Shoshonis, and Arikaras as scouts to help them fight the angry Sioux and Cheyenne. The Crow chief Plenty Coups was a famous warrior who took many Sioux scalps. Disunity among the Indian tribes helped the whites.

coming to an end. They must now go to small reservations, take up farming on 160 acres apiece, obey their white agents, or die.

The Indians' plains had by this time shrunk to parts of Montana and the western half of the Dakotas, and this they would have to give up, too. Many tribes had already gone to the reservations. Even such a famous chief as Red Cloud, who had forced the army to retreat from the Bozeman Trail, and who had counted more than eighty coups in war, admitted that further resistance was useless and bowed to the inevitable.

How did these reservations come into being? In order to "control the aborigines" and to solve once and for all the "vexing Indian problem," special areas called reservations had been set aside for the

Indians. All other land was to be opened to white settlers. A reservation usually came about in the following way. A final treaty would be signed with a tribe. By this treaty the Indians gave up all their land, and all future claims to it, in return for a reservation and protection by the government. Once on a reservation, a tribe was not supposed to leave, except for single individuals who had some business outside. Before 1900, when the rules were eased, even these few persons would often need a special permit from their white agent before they could leave. On the other hand, the reservations were to be safe from the encroachment of white settlers.

The whole process started in the 1850s with a number of treaties and preliminary agreements. It was finally made official by an act of Congress on March 3, 1871. By the early 1900s, there were 161 different reservations established throughout the United States. Some reservations were tiny, only a few acres in size, not larger than a fair-to-middling farm. The Navajo reservation, on the other hand, was so huge that one or two New England states could have been comfortably placed within its borders. Very large reservations were usually a sign that they suffered from a lack of water and that much of the land was worthless.

As far as the Indians of the Plains were concerned, most of their reservations were established in the years of 1868 and 1869. Generally a reservation lay within a tribe's former hunting grounds, but sometimes Indians were removed to places far from their homes. In other cases, two or three tribes were forced to share one reservation. It did not matter to the government if the tribes had been enemies or spoke different languages. They just would have to learn to get along with each other. Often, a reservation had a fort or army post at its center. That way it was easier to control the tribes.

Thus, in Colorado, a reservation had been created for the Ute. In Montana, the Blackfoot Indians were given a place around Browning.

The Crow warrior Spotted Rabbit is dressed in the same manner as Custer's scouts. He wears the characteristic hairstyle of the Crows.

In the same state, Gros Ventres and Assiniboins lived on the Fort Belknap Reservation, while other Assiniboins had to live at Fort Peck, together with their former enemies, the Brulé, Santee, and some Hunkpapa and Yanktonai Sioux. The Crow had been established at the Crow Agency and a place had been set aside for the Cheyenne near Lame Deer and Busby, Montana. In North Dakota, the Arikara,

Hidatsa, and Mandan were concentrated at Fort Berthold, while more of the warlike Hunkpapa Sioux were settled for good, so it was hoped, at Standing Rock. Oklahoma became a vast dumping ground for Indians unwanted in other, often faraway, places. In South Dakota, the sedentary Sioux tribes had been given the Yankton, Lower Brulé, and Crow Creek reservations, while their fierce western cousins were growing restless at the Pine Ridge, Rosebud, and Cheyenne River agencies. Finally, the Shoshone and Arapaho had to share the Wind River Reservation in Wyoming.

Before some of the last and most famous Indian battles took place, many tribes had already been forced to "walk the white man's road." But some chiefs with their followers would have nothing to do with the white men. They had withdrawn into the Powder River and Big Horn country, the last, large region which was as yet untouched, unfenced, unplowed. It was a region without a single settler and still had plenty of fat buffalo waiting to be hunted. Out there, in that vast land of rolling hills, were the "hostile" Cheyenne and Sioux. They still had ponies to ride and arms to fight with. Among these proud people, determined to defend their way of life to their last breath, were haughty chiefs like Crazy Horse, Gall, Two Moons, Crow King, Rain-in-the-Face, and American Horse. The great Sitting Bull spoke for them all when he said, "The Great Spirit has not made me a Reservation Indian!"

19 ▪ WHOSE LAST STAND?

It's a good day to die,
it's a good day to fight,
cowards to the rear,
Strong Hearts follow me!

CRAZY HORSE

Custer had it coming—
so do some others!

MODERN BUMPERSTICKER
SOLD ON RESERVATIONS

In the winter of 1875, the Secretary of the Interior gave an ultimatum to the Indians: "Give yourself up by January 31, 1876. Everybody found off the reservation after that date will be considered an enemy and treated accordingly."

Many circumstances combined to bring on the last war of resistance. The weather was terrible, and the message to "come in or else" could not be delivered to many isolated winter camps. There was nothing to eat on the reservations because the supplies, as usual, were either late in coming or stolen on the way. Many young men were disillusioned with reservation life. "This is for old people who have given up hope," they said as they rode off to join Crazy Horse and Sitting Bull.

When spring came, the Indians were busy hunting and feeding themselves, being joined all the time by their young brothers from the reservations. Most Indians were entirely ignorant of the deadline. The tribes had, in any case, given up paying much attention to the contradictory and forever-changing white man's orders and demands, which they could neither read nor understand.

The Paha Sapa—the Black Hills—were sacred to the Sioux Indians. A treaty had promised them this beautiful land forever—for as long as there would be a sun and a moon to shine upon it. General Custer led an expedition into the Black Hills, thereby breaking the treaty. He sent out the word: "There is gold in the grassroots!" Soon the Black Hills were overrun with frantic gold-hunters. This brought on the last great Indian battles.

The Indians bothered nobody, and nobody bothered them. There was not one white man in all the Big Horn and Powder River country. It was theirs to hunt as they pleased, to hunt the buffalo as they had done for as long as men could remember. They had the right and a pile of treaties signed by the Great White Father, to prove it.

The Sioux and Cheyenne did not want to fight, not even Crazy Horse and Sitting Bull. All they wanted was to be left alone. They were unaware of the huge forces brought together by rail, wagon, and paddle steamer and directed from far away by telegraph messages—forces that would converge upon them from all directions in one last, gigantic hunt in which the U.S. Army would be the hunter and the Indians would be the game.

The outcome of this hunt was possibly decided by the thoughts agitating the mind of one strong-willed man, George Armstrong Custer. Custer was under a cloud. He had accused a member of President Grant's family of corruption. He had testified to that effect before Congress, but he had only offered gossip and hearsay.

The president was furious, and Custer was in disgrace. He had been relieved of his command, and only the pleas of his old friends Sheridan and Terry, not to take his regiment away from him on the eve of battle, made it possible for him to ride at the head of his troopers.

He knew that his military career was nearing its end. He would be disgraced and dismissed. Soon he would be forgotten. But if it were he who won the last great victory over the Indians, even Grant would not dare to touch him. His fame would outshine that of all others, and the people might elect him president. He would have his battle and he would win it alone!

The army had mustered the largest force ever assembled in the Plains for one last "round-up." Three columns of troops were to enter the last remaining stronghold of the Indians from different directions, driving the "hostiles" before them. As the ring closed and the columns met, the Indians would be trapped and either taken prisoners or annihilated.

General Alfred H. Terry was in overall command of the operation. The three columns were led by Generals Crook, Gibbon, and Custer. At their last meeting, Terry offered Custer two quick-firing Gatling guns and reinforcements from another regiment. Custer rejected both. The guns would slow him up, and the Seventh Cavalry was strong enough to tackle all the Indians in the whole world. Grattan, Fetterman, and now Custer—history was about to repeat itself. Custer had orders to conform to an overall plan and not to attack the Indians without the support of the other columns, unless cornered.

As Custer rode off with his Seventh Cavalry, Terry called after him, "Now, Custer, don't be greedy! Wait for us!" Twisting in his saddle, Custer flashed his famous smile and shouted back, "No, I won't!" It was an answer that could be taken in two ways.

The Indians, too, had assembled in a larger force than ever before. They were not yet aware of the danger threatening them, but their experience of the last few years had taught them not to take any chances. No longer did they move in single bands. They were uneasy and thought there would be safety in numbers. All the Seven Council Fires of the western Sioux were represented: the Hunkpapa, the Brulé, the Oglala, the Without Bow, the Miniconjou, the Sihasapa, and the Two Kettle. With them were their trusted allies, the Cheyenne. Their camp circles stretched for miles, and their warriors filled the valley.

It made their hearts glad to see how many thousands had left the reservations, disobeying their white agents, in order to join their brothers on the plains. Here, for the last time, was the power and the glory of the tribes in all its savage splendor: the coup sticks wrapped in otter fur, the feathered command staffs, the war shirts, the sashes, the breast plates of polished bone, and the trailing war bonnets of the chiefs. At night innumerable campfires glowed as the throbbing of drums called the people to a dance or to a feast. It was good to see this once more, even if one had to die for it.

Near the present town of Busby, Montana, in the middle of a rancher's grazing land, rises a cluster of rocks covered with many scratched-in designs of human and animal figures. They were called Medicine Elk Rocks and were sacred to the Sioux and Cheyenne. Here the assembled tribes held their sun dance. Sitting Bull made a flesh offering by having fifty small pieces of skin cut from each of

The famous Sitting Bull was not a fighting war-chief, but a spiritual leader and holy man. He united the tribes for a last defense of their ancestral lands. After the final battles he became for a short time a circus performer in Buffalo Bill's Wild West Show. Annie Oakley, the famous trick-shooter, remembered that most of the money he made went into the pockets of small raggedy boys in New York and elsewhere. But most people remember Sitting Bull as the man whose wisdom helped to defeat Custer.

his arms. As he gazed at the sun, he fell into a trance and received his vision: many soldiers falling backwards into the Indians' camp and a voice whispering to him "I give you these, because they have no ears!"

Custer, in the meantime, followed his own vision of winning the battle that would make him president. He did not know it, but already the pincers that were designed to crush the Indians had been broken apart. At the Rosebud River, General Crook had met the Indians under Crazy Horse and he had been whipped. There were too many Sioux and Cheyenne for his taste, and he retired to his base.

Custer followed an ever-widening trail. It was the biggest his scouts had even seen. Travois poles had churned up the prairie for a

During the last Indian campaigns, Chief Red Cloud, who had fought the white soldiers for so many years, stayed peacefully on the Pine Ridge Reservation. He had decided that further fighting had become hopeless. But his son, Jack Red Cloud, joined the warriors and lost his warbonnet to some Shoshoni and Crow scouts. It was a thing hard to live down.

width of three miles. At last he came to a lookout with a distant view of the whole Little Bighorn valley. It was covered with the haze of a thousand campfires. The Crow and Arikara scouts saw the prairie quiver with a dark, squirming mass shrouded in purple dust. This was the enormous pony herd of the Indians, some fifteen thousand animals. "Look for worms!" said the scouts, pointing to the distant wiggling mass of horses. Custer could see nothing. His eyes were good, but not as good as those of the scouts. "If you don't find more Indians in that valley than you ever saw before," said Mitch Bouyer, the Chief of Scouts, "you can hang me!" The Crows burst into an eerie wail. They were singing their death song. The general was afraid of only one thing: that the Indians would "skedaddle" and run away.

It was the morning of the 25th of June, 1876. The wind had blown down the regimental pennon fluttering before the general's

At the Rosebud River the Indians, led by Crazy Horse and other famous chiefs, defeated General Crook and forced him to retreat. This enabled them to turn their whole strength against Custer, who attacked their camp at the Little Bighorn a few days later.

tent. One man put it up again, but it was immediately blown down for the second time. It was not only the Indians who believed in bad omens. Many of the officers looked grim. It was still dark when the regiment moved out. The mule train with its ammunition boxes soon fell behind. Custer rushed on. He was obsessed by the fear that the Indians would escape him. He was still not convinced that his scouts had seen the main Indian camp from the lookout, even though he knew they had better eyes than his. He sent Captain Benteen on a wild-goose chase to search the side canyons. No hostile must be allowed to get away. This weakened the regiment, as over one hundred men went with Benteen, but Custer rushed on.

At last he saw tepees. It was the camp circle of the Hunkpapa,

Chief Two Moons was one of the Cheyenne leaders at both the Rosebud and the Little Bighorn fights. The great warrior was blind when this picture was taken.

Sitting Bull's people. Custer did not know that this was only one of several large camp circles strung out along the Little Bighorn River. The river at this place formed many loops, and Custer could not see what lay beyond the first one. The Indians, on their part, were unaware of Custer's approach. They had just beaten Crook on the Rosebud and could not believe that more than one army was pursuing them. They had watched Crook retreat and, feeling safe at last, had spent the last few nights dancing and singing victory songs.

Custer told his second in command, Major Marcus Reno, to attack the village with three companies, about 130 men. The general would ride on and hit the Indians from behind to prevent their skedaddling. He told Reno that he would be supported by the whole outfit. Then Custer disappeared into the bluffs. The last Reno saw of him was a small figure in buckskins appearing for a brief moment on top of a distant hill, waving his white, broad-brimmed hat. He had with him about 220 men, all that was left after dividing his regiment again and again.

Reno lined up his three troops for a charge. The bugles blared as the horses broke into a gallop. There was a moment of panic in the Hunkpapa circle. Mothers hurried to get their children to a safe place, warriors grabbed their arms, and some even stopped to paint themselves and to put on their best clothing. Crazy Horse and Gall rallied the warriors with their war cries: "It's a good day to die, it's a good day to fight!" Sitting Bull did not take part in this battle, except to encourage the warriors. He was still weakened by his flesh sacrifice and had also, by this time, become a spiritual leader of his people rather than a war chief.

As more and more warriors swarmed out to oppose him, Reno got worried. Here were more Indians than he had ever dreamed of, and where was the "whole outfit" to support him? The worst of it was the nagging thought which he could not get out of his mind— was he another Major Elliott, to be sacrificed and abandoned? He decided to play it safe, dismounted his troops, and formed a skirmish line among the cottonwoods of the river bank. The Indians, seeing Reno hesitate, attacked him boldly.

A shot killed a scout next to Reno, spattering him with his blood. Reno was unnerved and ordered a retreat to the protecting hills across the river. He was the first to mount and flee. His men panicked and stampeded after him. Many were left behind in the timber. It was every man for himself and the devil take the hindmost. The Indians raced their horses alongside the troopers and clubbed them down. "It was like hunting buffalo," they said later. It was not the red warriors who were skedaddling on this day!

When Reno was finally able to make his stand on top of a hill, he had lost more than a third of his men. It did not seem as if he

There are many romantic pictures of Custer's Last Stand showing the General—saber in hand, his long locks flying in the wind, the last man to fall. Actually, nobody had a saber at the Little Bighorn and nobody knows at what stage of the battle Custer died. Also, the General who was known to the Indians at one time as Chief Long Hair was getting bald and wore whatever hair he had left short-cropped when he fought his last battle.

would be able to hold out for long, but the great mass of warriors before him suddenly wheeled off and raced downriver, disappearing in a great cloud of dust. A few skirmishers remained to harass the badly shaken major, who began to take big swallows from a bottle of whiskey which he had in his hip pocket. At last Captain Benteen and his men came back from their futile search for hostiles and joined the major on his hill. "For God's sake, help me," Reno blurted out. Benteen took charge of the defense. He was soon reinforced by the mule train with its large escort and load of ammunition boxes. At last all the detachments of the regiment had joined up with each other again, all, that is, except the five companies with Custer.

From the far distance, hidden in dust and smoke, came the echo of a tremendous fusillade. Shot followed upon shot so quickly that it

The Crow scout Curly was possibly the last man to see Custer alive. He survived the battle and brought to the outside world the first news that Custer's famous luck had finally run out.

was impossible to detect any pause. All that the men with Benteen and Reno could hear was one continuous ripple of sound, "like the tearing of a great blanket," as the Indians later described it.

Custer used to compare himself to Murat, the famous cavalry leader of the Napoleonic Wars. As the officers on Reno Hill listened to the distant volleys which grew fainter and finally ceased, one of them said: "I wonder what the Murat of the American Army is doing now?"

The last time any of the white survivors of the battle saw Custer was when he waved his hat at Reno's men from the top of the bluffs. He was probably looking for a gully leading down to the river, so that he could cross it a little farther down to take the Indians between two fires. As he rode on, he must have soon reached a spot from which the whole valley with the immense hostile camp, not just the Hunkpapa village, was visible. It was only now that Custer finally saw what he was up against. He could see thousands of Indians before him and he had only 220 men. If he at last realized that he was doomed, there was nothing he could do about it. He had come too far to retreat.

The Indians, too, were surprised. First there had been Crook. Then, at this very moment, they were battling Reno, and here was still another bunch of Long Knives to attack them. As the warriors massed to oppose this new enemy, five single Cheyennes rode far ahead to be the first to count coup. They wanted to do a deed that would be remembered, and it has not been forgotten to this day. As the chiefs who had been fighting Reno's troops a few miles away heard of this new force of soldiers, they wheeled to lead their warriors against this greater threat. It was this move which saved Reno. Custer was forced back from the river and up into the hills. His troopers, too, dismounted to form a firing line. As their carbines grew hot, the soft brass cartridges got stuck in the barrels. In this fight the bows and arrows of the Indians were the better weapons.

The end came fast. Attacked from all sides by overwhelming numbers, Custer and his men were killed to the last man. A horse named Comanche was the only living thing to survive. Paintings of the Custer fight show the general as the last man on his feet, his trusted six-shooter in his left hand, his flashing saber in his right, his golden locks waving around his shoulders. Actually, nobody in the regiment carried a saber because they had become obsolete. The Indians did not even bother to take Custer's scalp, as his hair was close-cropped and he was getting bald.

The commands of Major Reno and Captain Benteen were eventually rescued by Terry and Gibbon. The Indians withdrew at their arrival; they had fought only because they were attacked. The Battle of the Little Bighorn, which is known also as Custer's Last Stand, was in reality the last stand of the Plains Indians. It was all so simple, if the generals had only thought of it. It was not necessary to risk one's life chasing the "red devils" all over the plains, only to see them escape again and again. A much safer and surer way was to destroy their natural food supply and starve them into surrender. Bullets had not done the trick, but hunger would.

20 ▪ WHERE HAVE ALL THE BUFFALO GONE?

*The Buffalo Hunters have done
more in the last two years
to settle the vexed Indian
Question, than the entire regular
army in the last thirty years.
They are destroying the Indians'
commissary.*

GENERAL PHILIP SHERIDAN

It was not the soldiers who defeated the Indians in the end but the buffalo hunters. It availed the Indians little to defend their hunting grounds when there was nothing left to hunt. Once the last buffalo herd was gone, even the bravest warrior had to become a reservation Indian or see his family starve. "The Buffalo Hunters are destroying the Indians' commissary," wrote General Sheridan. "Send them powder and lead, if you will, and let them kill, skin, and sell until they have exterminated the buffalo. Then your prairies will be covered with speckled cattle and the festive cowboy, who follows the hunter as a second forerunner of civilization!"

It was all very simple. Shortly after the Civil War came "the iron snake" and the "talking wire," the railroad and the telegraph. The trains brought the hunters to the Plains and the skins back to the leather manufacturers. First to arrive were the sportsmen, lured by ads and posters such as this:

RAILWAY EXCURSION AND BUFFALO HUNT!

An excursion train will leave Leavenworth at 8 A.M. for Sheridan on Tuesday, October 27, 1868, and return on Friday. Ample time will be had for a GRAND BUFFALO HUNT ON THE PLAINS. Buffaloes are so numerous along the road that they are shot from cars every day. All passengers can have refreshments on the cars at reasonable prices. Round trip ten dollars only!

Buffalo Skinners - Taking the Monster's Robe in Montana Jan 1882

In 1850, some forty million buffalo had roamed the Great Plains. By 1883 they were gone. They were killed for their hides, which sold for as low as one dollar apiece. One hunter shot 263 animals during one day at the rate of three per minute. Each hunter kept three or four skinners busy. They took only the hide and left the meat to rot.

Soon the rotting carcasses of thousands of buffalo were lying along the rails, "rendering the plains pestilencial," as one of the "sportsmen" complained. What really doomed the buffalo was a new tanning process by which hides could be mass converted into good shoe and belt leather at $3.50 the skin.

Unsuccessful miners and homesteaders, drifters, and vagabonds went into the profitable buffalo-killing business. The supply was so great that in 1873, the price dropped to sixty cents per hide. One had to slaughter an awful lot of buffalo to make, in the truest sense of the word, a "killing" in this gruesome market.

The typical buffalo hunter was recognizable by his rawhide coat stiff with blood and gore and a stink about him that no amount of scrubbing could get off. As one English traveler commented, "He made a very unsatisfactory companion on a stage coach." These were General Sheridan's forerunners of civilization.

Indians had killed the buffalo with bows and arrows. It was their main source of food. The army supported the white hunter who killed buffalo for profit. Once the buffalo was gone, the Indians would have to surrender or starve.

A hunter could shoot about 100 buffaloes from a single spot. One man shot 263 animals during one working day at the rate of three per minute. In 1882 the agent at the Standing Rock Reservation helped a man named Dickinson to kill 5,000 buffaloes in two days, forcing the Indians to assist in this slaughter. A good hunter could keep a team of four or five skinners busy. The constant blast of their rifles made many of them permanently deaf.

When the hunters had finally killed the last buffalo, some clever men still found a way to make a profit from their bones, which littered the prairie as far as the eye could see. Bones brought $2.50 per ton. They were made into buttons and combs in busy factories or ground up to make a fertilizer which was rich in phosphates. This gave rise to a new profession, the lowly, looked-down-upon "bone picker." Sometimes Indians did this work to earn a few pennies. One can imagine how they felt as they gathered up the remains of the

After being near extinction at the beginning of this century, the buffalo is making a comeback in America's national and state parks. There are even some ranches which raise good-sized herds. These herds have to be thinned out from time to time to avoid overgrazing. Chief Lame Deer is shown here with buffalo heads from recently killed animals. Tourists can again order buffalo steak and buffaloburgers in some western restaurants. Buffalo tastes delicious—like first-class beef, and meat from the hump is particularly tender.

animal which was sacred to them, which had furnished them everything that they needed to live.

In 1830, an estimated 75 million buffaloes had roamed the Plains. In 1850, there were still close to 50 million left. By 1883, there were none. The buffalo were gone so quickly that many Indians could simply not believe that the white man had killed them all. "The buffalo people have gone away into a big cave," Sioux mothers told their children. "They will return, once the white hunters have left." But the buffalo did not return.

It is only thanks to great luck and the devotion of a handful of men that a few animals were saved and the species did not become altogether extinct, as did the dodo bird and the passenger pigeon.

In 1886, the National Museum in Washington sent out its taxidermist, William Hornaday, to find six, fine specimens for a buffalo group exhibit. He discovered, to his horror, that there were only about eight survivors left in all of the Dakotas and nobody knew exactly where to find them. He searched for more than half a year and finally came upon a spot in northern Montana which had been overlooked by the hunters. It was a forbidding area, where the earth was split into innumerable cracks so that "one couldn't slow-walk a horse through it." Another place where a few buffaloes survived was in the Cariboo Mountains of Canada. The hunters had not thought that there were buffalo that far north. An Indian named Walking Coyote had gone to Alberta and driven a herd of thirty animals across the border into the Flathead Reservation of Montana. In 1908, the National Bison Range was established on some twenty thousand acres of the Flathead Reservation. It is symbolic, and more than just an accident, that an Indian and an Indian reservation played an important part in the saving of the buffalo, so that today white tourists can gaze at a herd in Yellowstone or Wind Cave National Park. They can even order a "buffaloburger" for lunch, as some surplus animals are again being killed at these places.

But as far as the Plains Indians were concerned, the buffalo had gone forever, together with a way of life, and the tribes were safely cooped up on the reservations. The main act was played out, but the tragedy was not quite ended.

21 ▪ WALKING THE WHITE MAN'S ROAD

*A reservation is a parcel of
land, inhabited by Indians
and surrounded by thieves.*

GENERAL WILLIAM SHERMAN

If some evil genie would take us by the scruff of the neck and
transport us into some strange world which we could neither understand nor leave, where we had to lead a life for which we were
utterly unprepared, and where everything we had been taught was
useless, we would find ourselves in the same situation that faced the
Indians on the reservations.

A man's life changed abruptly from the first moment he became a
reservation Indian. Once he had been proud to be a skilled hunter
who provided his family with plenty of food. Now his horses and his
gun had been taken away, and he was not even allowed to leave the
reservation to look for game. It didn't matter anyhow, for the buffalo,
the elk, and the antelope were gone.

A man had been brought up to be a warrior. Only by counting
coup could he win the love of a woman or the respect of his tribe.
But the days of happy raiding were gone, like the buffalo. The warrior societies, too, had vanished. There was no reason to have them
any more. Once a proud provider, the Indian had become a beggar
waiting for a government hand-out. The food that was given him
was not the kind he was used to. Often it was spoiled, and nearly
always he got only a small part of what had been promised him.
Then he and his family starved.

A Plains Indian had striven to make a name for himself by his
generosity. He had been praised for giving away blankets and horses

to the helpless ones and for inviting his friends to a feast. Now he had nothing left to give.

The women, also, were sad, as time trickled by much too slowly and without joy. Those who were once praised by their husbands for their skills in tanning a hide or decorating a fine war shirt were now idle.

Good white men, who wanted to help the Indians, often harmed them instead. Missionaries and philanthropists thought that all the problems could be solved by giving the Indians a plot of land, some seed corn, and a few farm implements. This would at once make them into prosperous, self-sufficient farmers. These good people forgot that the land set aside for the Indians was in most cases unsuitable for raising crops. They also ignored the fact that the Indians were brought up to look upon farming as women's work, shameful for a man to do even in some tribes that had at one time practiced agriculture.

Their religion often forbade them to rip up and despoil their Mother, the Earth, by digging and plowing. Land belonged to all people, and it was a bad thing to fence it in and to claim that it belonged to this or that person. Some white agents made the Indians work the land even when dust storms and dry spells destroyed their crops. This was to "teach the Indian to work hard, like a white man." This made the Indians detest farming more than ever.

Cattle raising was more to the Indians' taste. It was the next best thing to hunting buffalo. A man did not have to be ashamed of running livestock. Consequently, the Indians took very good care of the first herds of cattle given to them. But a few terrible years of drought brought famine to the reservations. The promised rations did not arrive and when there was nothing else to eat, the Indians slaughtered the cattle. They even killed their few remaining horses, with the women singing the death song for the brave ponies, weeping as for a dead relative.

A man's life changed abruptly from the first moment he became a reservation Indian. The government agents tried to make the warriors into farmers, but reservation soil was poor and crops failed. The Indians also disliked farming because they believed that land belonged to all men and should not be owned individually or fenced in.

The government people nodded their heads wisely and said "I told you so!" They were angry at the good-for-nothing savages, who had eaten the cattle given to them at the taxpayer's expense.

Tribal government was also badly affected. A man no longer rose to be a chief in the old, natural way. Those who did what the white agent wanted became chiefs and were given fine, two-story houses, so that everybody could see that it payed to do as one was told. Those who disobeyed were removed from office. The old nomadic democracy of the Plains vanished. The whole attitude of the government was summed up by Hiram Price, U.S. Commissioner of Indian Affairs, in the 1880s: "To domesticate and civilize wild Indians is a noble work. But to allow them to drag along, year after year, in their old superstition, laziness, and filth instead of elevating them in the scale of humanity would be a lasting disgrace."

It sounded more like a circus trainer teaching a lion to jump

The trading stores demanded high prices for inferior goods. Some also sold whisky, even where this was illegal.

through a flaming hoop than a government official trying to help an uprooted and bewildered people. It also overlooked the fact that before the coming of the white man, Indians had not been filthy, drunken, lazy, or diseased, and that some of the white agents, traders, and ranchers needed a lot more civilizing than the red man.

Progress, as the white man understood it at the time, also meant the destruction of the Indians' old religion. In 1883 the government made rules to "do away with demoralizing and barbarous customs." Many old beliefs and rites were now called "Indian offenses" and were treated as crimes. Give-away feasts, the sun dance, the time-hallowed way of burying the dead, even the building of a sweat lodge, were now punishable by a jail sentence.

Episcopalians, Catholics, Quakers, and Presbyterians established churches and schools. They competed with each other. The mission-aries did not understand how wrong it was to deprive the Indians of their religion, their language, and their culture. The Indians had seen the buffalo killed and their land taken away. Now some men tried to take away their souls. They would not succeed, but it was not because they did not try.

Just as the Christian faith had once been practiced secretly in the catacombs, so the Indian religion went underground. It was stubborn and refused to die. Persecution only made it stronger. Hidden from the eyes of the missionaries, old men instructed their grandchildren in the ancient ways and told them to "keep the flame burning, to pass it on."

After many years, the attitude of the government changed with the belated admission that freedom of religion was also meant for Indians. And so the chant of medicine men is heard once more on the reservations, as the old customs are being practiced again openly. It is not surprising that the young militants have a special interest in the old faith. It helps them to find their identity and expresses their Indianness. Many civil rights protests open with a prayer by a medicine man. The young people occupying Mount Rushmore to draw attention to a number of Indian grievances invited Chief Lame Deer to come up to their camp site to perform a religious ceremony, to say a prayer for the success of their enterprise. A poster hanging in the office of an Indian civil rights organization reads: "Notice to white men: the Great Spirit is alive and well in South Dakota."

22 ▪ WOUNDED KNEE

I come to tell news
I come to tell news
The buffaloes are coming again
The buffaloes are coming again
My father tells.
The Dead People are coming again
The Dead People are coming again
My father tells.
The earth will be made new
The earth will be made new
Says the Mother.

GHOST DANCE SONG

Men cannot live without hope. In their utter despair, the Indians waited for some miracle to rescue them from their misery. In 1889, an eclipse frightened them. For a moment it seemed as if the sun would disappear like the buffalo. But the shadow passed, and the sun went on shining.

Soon afterwards wonderful news spread from tribe to tribe. Far away, in the southern plains, a great medicine man had appeared. He preached a new creed of hope and comfort. The Great Spirit had taken pity on his Indian children, and he would make a new world. A great flood would come, and the earth would roll itself up like a giant carpet. Rolled up would be the "iron snake" and the "whispering wire," the ugly smelters and mine dumps, the fences and the stinking new animals (pigs and sheep), the filthy towns with their saloons and gambling houses. Underneath would appear the new, happy world that the Great Spirit intended for his children, forever green and unspoiled.

To these new plains would return the departed ones, the dead

In 1890 the ghost dance spread throughout the Plains tribes. Dancers dropped in a faint from exhaustion as they went on singing and dancing for hour after hour. By doing so they hoped to bring back both the buffalo and their dead relatives killed by the white man.

ancestors, the parents and children killed by war and famine. The tribes would live in peace and make war no more. The white man would disappear, go back to his faraway lands across the Big Water, or simply be rolled up. It did not matter which.

All the Indians needed to do to bring this new world about was to dance the ghost dance, which the prophet would teach them. They would have to dance each month for four days. Also one must always wear a feather, so that the Great Spirit could tell at a glance whom to save and whom to roll up. If they did this, all would come to pass as foretold within two years, by the end of 1890.

The prophet's name was Wovoka, called the Red Messiah by

some white men. He was a Paiute Indian and lived near Walker Lake in southwestern Nevada. For a number of years, he had worked for a white farmer who read the Bible aloud to his household after dinner. Wovoka's new creed was therefore a mixture of Indian and Christian beliefs.

In the old days, the warlike northern tribes would not have been impressed by the teachings of a Paiute, a tribe they used to look down upon. But things were different now. Even the proud Sioux and Cheyenne were like women, huddling in the shade of the trading posts. The Kiowa, the Arapaho, the Shoshone, and the Cheyenne

This old painted hide shows an Arapaho ghost dance. One dancer has fallen down in a trance.

began to perform the ghost dance. Two Sioux warriors, Short Bull and Kicking Bear, decided to visit Wovoka. They had to do so secretly and ride for many days and nights without being seen by white settlers.

They finally arrived at Wovoka's home. The prophet taught them the ghost dance and they fell into a trance. They told the story later:

"A big Eagle carried them over the clouds to a happy place, with villages such as they had before the white man came. Everything there was beautiful. Nothing could be seen that was of the white man's making. No guns and no whiskey existed in this beautiful land. Wakan Tanka, the Great Spirit, called for the dead parents and friends of the Sioux envoys to show themselves. The dead came riding on their finest horses, in white, shining garments of deerskin, dazzling to behold. Around them, as far as the eye could see, were herds of elk and buffalo. The Great Spirit told them that the earth was old and worn out, ruined by the white man's greed. If the tribes would follow Wovoka's instructions, the beautiful land would become a reality and the dead would return."

As the Sioux came out of their trances, tears were streaming down their faces. They hastened to bring the good tidings back to their tribe. Men and women were given ghost dance shirts with designs on them that would make them bulletproof, in case the whites interfered and attacked the dancers. The people were taught the words and the melodies they would have to remember. They were taught how to dance in a circle, men and women holding hands, facing always towards the center. They had only their own voices to accompany them, because this was a dance without drums or any other instruments. And so they danced, hour after hour, without food or water, until they dropped in a dead faint. Sometimes a dancer broke out of the circle, his arms outstretched towards the horizon, his eyes closed, trembling, seeing with his inward eyes the vision of the promised land.

As taught by Wovoka, the new religion was entirely peaceful. He did not teach the destruction of the whites, only that they would go away. The new world could not be brought about by bloodshed. Even among the warlike tribes, no violence was contemplated. Why expose oneself to slaughter and suffering, said the leaders, when the new world will come by itself?

But the ranchers and homesteaders were worried. To the white people living around the reservations, the ghost dance seemed to be the forerunner of a general uprising. Alarming newspaper stories began to appear, first in the Western and then in the Eastern press. Government officials who read these articles became worried. They ordered the agents who were in charge of the reservations to suppress the ghost dance, using their Indian police force.

Most local officials knew that there was a time limit involved. Wovoka had said that the new world would come by the end of 1890. Why he fixed that date nobody knows. Maybe the eclipse, which had made a big impression upon him, had something to do with it. In the 1840s, a white preacher in New York State had prophesied the end of the world for a certain day. Many sober New Yorkers sold all their belongings, put on white nightshirts, and climbed trees to await zero hour from a convenient perch. These were educated, mostly well-to-do people, not illiterate, starving Indians. At any rate, the Indians believed that the new earth would come by the end of 1890 or never. All the officials had to do was let the Indians dance until the deadline passed. Then the new religion would collapse by itself. Level-headed men also pointed out that not one single white man had been killed as a result of the ghost dance.

Unfortunately, Agent Royer, at the Pine Ridge Reservation of South Dakota, was not a man of strong nerves. Two thousand of his Sioux had moved out into the almost inaccessible Badlands, where they danced the ghost dance. They slaughtered a few of the white rancher's cattle that came their way and cursed Royer when he ordered them back. Royer remembered a day, fourteen years before, when these same Sioux—the fierce Oglala, Crazy Horse's tribe—had also bolted their reservation to join their chief at the Little Bighorn. The thought made Royer lose his head. He sent out a call for troops to protect him and the white settlers. Soon eight thousand soldiers surrounded the Sioux reservations, among them the Seventh Cavalry with many veterans from the Custer battle. The army lost no time in searching the country for bands of ghost dancers, trying to persuade, and if necessary, force them to return to the Pine Ridge and adjacent Rosebud reservations. While the situation was danger-ous, no open clashes occurred at or near these two reservations, which were situated in the southwestern corner of South Dakota along the Nebraska border. While soldiers and Indians confronted each other nervously, the scene of the ghost dance drama shifted temporarily to the north.

Agent McLaughlin at Standing Rock had not lost his nerve. He knew that the ghost dance constituted no danger. It did not bother him, but Sitting Bull did. The old chief embodied the spirit of the old way of life. He thwarted and defied McLaughlin at every step. As long as Sitting Bull remained free to influence his people, McLaugh-lin could not make docile farmers out of the Hunkpapa. The agent's goal in life was to "civilize" the Sioux, to make them act like white men. This, he thought, was their only salvation. Sitting Bull was in his way. There could not be two chiefs at Standing Rock, McLaugh-lin decided, but only one—himself.

In the ghost dance trouble, McLaughlin saw a chance to rid him-self of his enemy. He wanted no troops. His problem consisted of one single man. He could handle this matter without help from the outside. McLaughlin reported that Sitting Bull was the moving force

The ghost dancers believed that they could cause the earth to roll up like a carpet with all the white man's ugly things: the roads and fences, mines and ranches, telegraph poles, and railroad tracks. Underneath would be once more the green, unspoiled prairie, teeming with game. As this modern photograph shows, the earth has not rolled up.

behind the ghost dance, which was not true. He obtained a written order for the chief's arrest and sent thirty-three Indian policemen, of whose loyalty he could be sure, to bring in Sitting Bull, dead or alive.

It was still dark when this force, commanded by Sergeant Red Tomahawk, surrounded Sitting Bull's pitiful shack on the morning of December 15, 1890. At first the old chief was willing to come peacefully, but as the police manhandled him and prodded him along, he became angry. Outside the little cabin, Sitting Bull's followers came rushing to the scene. The high, trilling war cry of the Sioux women filled the air and a voice sang out:

> *"Sitting Bull,*
> *You were a warrior, once.*
> *What are you going to do?"*

The old chief struggled to get free. Immediately the police and Sitting Bull's men began to fight. A savage gun battle raged at close quarters. Among the chief's followers were his closest relatives and comrades in arms. Among the police were men who had always opposed him. McLaughlin had picked them for that very reason. The Sioux have a saying: "Fighting soldiers and Crow is one thing, but watch out when Sioux fights Sioux! Then you'll really know what fighting is!" When it was over, fifteen men were dead or dying, among them Sitting Bull. The chief's fifteen-year-old son was killed by the police in revenge for their own dead.

The news of their leader's death crushed the Sioux. The year of 1890 was almost over, and the earth had not rolled up. At Pine Ridge and Rosebud the Indians were surrounded by thousands of troops. Fearful and dejected, they came home to surrender. Within the large Pine Ridge Reservation lies the town and administrative center of the same name. Here was the house of old Chief Red Cloud, who was considered a friend of the whites. Here the various groups of ghost dancers assembled, seeking the protection of Red Cloud, showing their peaceful intentions by giving up the few rusted, ancient guns still in their possession.

Among the last, haggard bands to return from the Badlands was that of Big Foot, an Oglala chief. He tried to find safety at the town of Pine Ridge, but the soldiers found him first. Dying of pneumonia,

This photograph of Wounded Knee, with the church, and an Indian tepee and sweatbath, is symbolic of two faiths and two races living side by side in peace.

Big Foot surrendered peacefully. He had the misfortune to fall into the hands of the Seventh Cavalry. Officers and men were revengeful and trigger-happy. They brought the Indians to a campsite near Wounded Knee, already well within the borders of the reservation.

Big Foot's group was surrounded by three thousand men. Guns were trained on them. Then their wagons and blankets were searched for weapons. A medicine man named Yellow Bird made the soldiers nervous by throwing dust at them and uttering war cries. A deaf-mute boy dropped and accidentally discharged an old rifle. This was the signal for a general massacre. The Indians had been disarmed. They did not even have a half dozen weapons left. Chief Big Foot was shot down in the soldiers' tent where he had been under medical care. The Hotchkiss guns were pouring shells into groups of women and children. Out of 250 Indians, 200 were killed, 62 of them mothers and children.

The soldiers had about sixty men killed and wounded, most of them by their own bullets. As the soldiers fired into the camp from opposite sides, they naturally hit many of their own comrades. The bodies of the Indians, frozen stiff into grotesque postures, were stacked up like corded wood and buried together in a ditch. A photographer took pictures. The soldiers would have souvenirs to send back to their families.

When it was all over, the men responsible for the tragedy were themselves horrified at what they had done. General Miles was furious and suspended the regiment's colonel. The general had no trouble persuading the Indians to go back to their homes. Now, when it was too late, it was found that the whole problem could have been solved without bloodshed. If the government had only waited a few more weeks, the ghost dance would have collapsed by itself, peacefully, when the new earth, promised by the prophet Wovoka, failed to appear on the predicted date. In the frozen snow at Wounded Knee, the dream of a beautiful new earth had come to an end.

23 ▪ THE NOT VANISHING RACE

*I want the White Man
with me, but not
to be my Chief.*

SITTING BULL

*The story of the American Indian
has been marked with the White
Man's frequent aggression, broken
agreements, intermittent remorse,
and prolonged failure.*

PRESIDENT RICHARD M. NIXON

Fifty years ago, there was much talk about the "vanishing race." It seemed at the time that the Indians would disappear like the buffalo and that the remnants of the tribes would be swallowed up by the much more numerous white population. Luckily, the Indians are no longer vanishing. Indian families have, on the average, more children than the rest of us and the number of people on the reservations is increasing steadily. From a low point at the beginning of the century, many tribes have grown to be as numerous as they were when the first white man met them. This is not true, though, for all. Tribes like the Pawnee, Hidatsa, and Mandan were so ravaged by smallpox that they have never been able to recover. Such tribes are reduced to a few hundred people, often not enough to have a reservation of their own. Sometimes two or three of these small tribes are thrown together in one small area and are not only fighting a grim struggle for their simple, physical survival, but also a losing battle for their tribal identity, language, and culture.

Even in the tribes which have regained much of their former population, the chances of a child living to manhood are much smaller than that of a white child. The average life span on a reservation is forty-three years, twenty years less than in the rest of the country.

The Indians' physical well-being is looked after by the U.S. Public Health Service, not by the Bureau of Indian Affairs. This is the only part of the Indians' life which is not in the charge of the all-powerful bureau. By and large, the Public Health Service has provided good hospitals and experienced, dedicated doctors. It has trained many Indian nurses and health aides. It is waging a successful fight against tuberculosis. Still, Indians die younger than whites and suffer from health problems which are unknown among white, middle-class families. The chief cause of such problems as malnutrition, and eye, ear, and skin diseases is often just plain poverty. Although the hospitals and doctors are good, they are far too few. The lines of Indian patients waiting to be treated are too long. An Indian's smile often reveals that he has few teeth left. The health service provides only one dentist for every three thousand Indians.

In 1966, Mr. John Wooden Legs, president of the Cheyenne tribe, put it this way: "White men die of heart disease and cancer, we still die of pneumonia, tuberculosis, and diphtheria. When we, too, will live long enough to die of heart disease and cancer, we'll know we have it made at last!"

In spite of these handicaps, the Indian has made a comeback in more ways than just numbers. As more and more people become aware of the "real Indian," of his problems, his culture, and his history, many old prejudices and misconceptions disappear. It is hard to say which attitude was worse: the Indian viewed as a murdering, bloodthirsty, yelping redskin—and, later, a loafing, drunken good-for-nothing—or the image of the noble savage, pure and undefiled, a kind of superhuman nature boy, untouched by the imperfections of modern civilization.

There are few jobs on reservations. Idle men sit near the tribal office waiting for something to turn up.

People tend to view all strangers as stereotypes: All Irishmen are red-headed, talkative, and love a fight; Italians sing all the time, eat spaghetti, and are carefree, lovable operatic tenors; all Germans drink beer, eat sausage, and do the goosestep. The less we know about a people, the more we are inclined to look upon them as stereotypes—and the outside world knew very little about the Indians.

Most people have gained their knowledge of Indians from movies and television. Several generations of white children have grown up with the image of a small, heroic band of whites successfully standing up to hordes of feathered fiends. The Indians made it easy for their enemies by riding stupidly around and around the whites until they were all shot dead. If there were too many Indians, the cavalry came to the rescue. As the bugle sounded the charge, hundreds of little white hands would clap in glee, but not even the well-known bugle call was authentic.

The Indians of today are trying to correct this stereotyped image. They are protesting discriminating films, ads, and toys which exploit Indians and show them in a false light. In many cities they picketed *A Man Called Horse,* a movie widely advertised as authentic, but in which the red hero was played by a Hawaiian, the young heroine by a Greek, and the old Indian grandmother by a white, Anglo-Saxon actress. The movie portrayed the Indians as Stone Age savages mainly occupied with killing each other in various messy ways.

Indians want to be seen and understood as they really are. They do not like to be depicted as savages; they do not want to be gushed over sentimentally; they do not want to be romanticized or viewed as living museum exhibits. George Catlin said over a hundred years ago that the Indian "is neither saint or savage."

Sioux, Cheyenne, Crow, Blackfeet—these are all white men's names. The real names of the tribes, spoken in their own languages, just mean "The People," "The Human Beings," and this is how they look upon themselves and how they want to be seen by others—*as people.*

Indians go to the same schools, vote in the same elections, and buy in the same supermarkets as everybody else. They are not simple-minded children of nature. They have to live and work in a modern society like other Americans. They have, however, certain special problems.

Lehman Brightman, a Sioux and a teacher of Indian studies, says: "We Indians have approximately 56 million acres of land left in this country, and the soil conservation people did a survey and found that out of 56 million acres, 14 million were severely eroded, 17 million were critically eroded, and 25 million were slightly eroded.

A reservation still means tarpaper shacks and dilapidated house trailers.

Which means we are the proud owners of 56 million acres of erosion!"

Farming, on most reservations, is not the answer to the Indians' problem. Much Indian land could be made productive by irrigation, but all too often the Indians find that even what little water they have left is threatened by being tapped for the use of white ranchers and farmers. In 1887, the Indian reservations still comprised 138 million acres; today there are only 56 million acres left. Water resources have shrunk in proportion. Pollution by industry and agriculture outside the reservation has further worsened the water situation.

Even the land that still legally belongs to the Indians is not used for their benefit. At Pine Ridge, South Dakota, the second largest reservation, only one per cent of the land is used by Indians. They can not obtain the necessary loans to have their own cattle. Consequently, most of the land is leased by white ranchers who reap the profit. The Indians get only the lease money which, in most cases, is set too low. The Bureau of Indian Affairs (BIA for short) does the bargaining for them, sets the rates and conditions, and holds the money in trust.

Even ecology is sometimes used as a weapon against the Indians. In the name of conservation, they are forbidden to fish and hunt on their own land without a license. On the other hand, conservation does not seem to apply to the many white amateur hunters and sports fishermen, who have the money to pay for licenses and who bring tourist dollars into the state.

To understand the Indians' problem it is best to look upon a reservation as a tiny, underdeveloped country. The whole concept under which the Bureau of Indian Affairs functioned was that the tribes were independent, foreign nations which were conquered in war and then occupied. This original concept is forgotten today, but it can still be faintly seen when one looks closely at the structure of reservation rule. Reservations are still colonies, with a general lack of industry which creates high unemployment. Funds are often lacking for the Indians to start their own enterprises which would create jobs and paychecks. Many people have to leave their home territory if they want to find work.

In theory, Indian tribes govern themselves. In the Plains, tribal elections are usually held every two years. Indians choose their tribal president and vice chairman, the tribal councilmen, and other officials. There are Indian courts with Indian judges and Indian policemen. But reservation government is really a form of dual government. Side by side with the tribal government exists the

Bureau of Indian Affairs. Its head is usually a white superintendent. He has many officials on his staff, also mostly white. In some places there are as many bureaucrats as there are Indians. As in an old-time African or Asian colony, there is the administration compound—a little oasis of neat streets, near bungalows, and well-tended lawns with sprinklers, all built and maintained at government expense. Only a hundred yards off, but a world apart, stands the "native city" of tar-paper shacks, tilting cabins, corroded house trailers, and unsanitary outhouses.

The dual government might be workable if it were not so lopsided. It is hard to exaggerate the power of the BIA. The tribal government is like a little toy poodle harnessed to a wagon together with the huge BIA oxen. It is easy to see that the wagon will go where the oxen goes and that the little toy poodle won't have much pull. The book *Our Brother's Keeper* explains it very well: "The Bureau is realtor, banker, teacher, social worker; it runs the employment service, vocational and job training program, contract office, chamber of commerce, highway authority, housing agency, police department, conservation service, water works, power company, telephone company, planning office. It is a land office, a land developer, patron of the arts, ambassador from and to the outside world, and also guardian, protector and spokesman." One can see that there is very little for the tribal council and its president to govern.

When the Indians gave up their land for reservations, they were given treaties promising them protection and the material means necessary for their existence. They want these treaties fulfilled. They must be fulfilled if Indians are to survive as INDIANS! The tribes would like the BIA to give up much of its power, to let Indians run its programs and take over for themselves many of the BIA's functions. Until that day arrives they want the bureau, that is the federal government, to protect their rights. Heavy-handed and humiliating

Houses on Indian reservations are often primitive—without running water, plumbing, or electricity.

as the rule of the BIA has been, it has functioned as the Indians' only shield against termination, a policy which often brings destruction for a tribe.

Termination in simple terms means that the government pays a tribe a compensation for its land and then washes its hands of it, abolishing the reservation and saying in effect: "We taught you all you need to know and paid for your land. Here are a couple of thousand dollars for each of you; now you can make it on your own and join the mainstream."

The Indian buys a car with the money and looks for work in a big city. After a few years the car comes to its natural end in some wrecking yard. The land is gone forever. The money is gone. The Indian is alone in a strange town, at a strange job, speaking a strange language, without his tribe and friends who would understand and help him. It is hard under these conditions to hold on to one's identity and values, to remain an Indian.

This happened to the Menominee of Wisconsin in 1961. Before termination they were well off, proud of their fine hospital and saw-mill. "You made good," said the government, "you are ready for termination. Congratulations." The Menominee were persuaded to exchange their reservation and the government's protection for money. Once paid, they were thus abandoned and their former reservation became the poorest county in Wisconsin. The state did not have the same amount of money to spend as had the BIA. Not only did the reservation lose its status as Indian land protected by the U.S. Government, but many of the individual Indian property owners lost their land when they couldn't pay the Wisconsin real estate taxes. "The Menominee payed a high price for being freed from the BIA's apron strings," says Robert Burnette, a Sioux civil rights leader. "The price was death."

All through the 1950s, under the Eisenhower administration, termination was the declared policy of the government. The hoped-for solution to all Indian problems was to have the Indians assimilate, or blend into the general population. Besides the Menominee, the Paiute in Utah were terminated. The Coleville Indians of Washington State still feel themselves threatened by the same fate. But most tribes have successfully withstood all attempts and cajoleries to be obliterated in this way.

Since then, official policy has changed. The government now admits that it has been wrong, that the tribes should keep their reservations and their identity, as the one cannot exist without the other. But the tribes remain skeptical. Administrations change and the termination policy could come back. Besides, there is a steady, hidden form of termination going on even now. It is called "relocation." An Indian unable to find work on the reservation is given a one-way bus ticket to a large city like Denver or Chicago. He is found some job, any job, and is then promptly forgotten. It is hoped that he will never return to be "a problem again" on the reservation.

And so the BIA continues to rule the Indians' lives, unloved and criticized by many Indians, but also necessary for their protection. Good, bad, or indifferent, the BIA remains the symbol of the government's good intentions to fulfill its obligations to the Indians, and it will have to do until something better comes along.

24 ▪ CIVIL RIGHTS NO MAN'S LAND

We used to call them
"House Indians,"
and "Uncle Tomahawks."
Now we call them "Apples,"
red outside, white inside.

DENNIS BANKS

Robert Burnette, former tribal president and director of the National Congress of American Indians, calls the reservations a "civil rights no man's land." Non-Indians tend to view the black man's and the red man's struggle for civil rights as very much the same thing. Indians are not too happy about this because, as they tell us, "There are similarities, but there are also great differences."

The similarities are obvious. Both races are suffering from discrimination. Both are poor. Their average income is much lower than that of their white fellow citizens. Their education is inferior. Many young Indian militants have borrowed the methods and vocabulary of the black civil rights struggle and adapted them to their own situation. This makes the seeming similarity even more obvious.

But differences in the situation of the two minorities are very great. Most Indians live on reservations—rural slums—in shacks that often have no running water, electricity, or plumbing. It is still a common sight to see an Indian boy with two pails making the long walk to the river to supply his family's daily needs of drinking and cooking water.

In the South, black sharecroppers have to live in the same primitive and isolated way. The difference is that most black people now live in city ghettos, most Indians still in a rural setting. Once an

Indian comes to live in the city, he is often treated like a black person. It is hard for him to find a place to live, even harder to pay for it once he has found it. A Sioux living in the town of Winner, South Dakota, has this to say: "We got no plumbing, just privies outdoors. I could afford a better home, but they have discrimination. They don't want an Indian for a neighbor. But I have changed my mind. It's no longer a question of whether he likes me, but whether I like him."

The white ranchers and the people in the small towns around the reservations discriminate against Indians because they have a bad conscience. As one Indian put it: "Those folks don't like us because they are all living on land stolen from us. They have a very questionable title to their real estate. They feel that our existence is a threat to them." The same man admitted that Indians were well treated, even made much of, in some the big cities—New York, San Francisco, Chicago, or Philadelphia. But he was quick to point out: "Those big city people are nice to us, but they are also patronizing. They look upon us as cultural curiosities and expect us to wear feathers and to dance for them."

There are welfare problems. Chief Lame Deer comments: "There are no jobs. We are like beggars in the street, we live from eight different kinds of hand-outs. Take one of them, ADC, aid to dependent children. An ADC mother makes more money by kicking her husband out. She doesn't want him back because then the money stops." In all this, Indians are not receiving any special favors. They are treated exactly as other welfare clients.

Reservation Indians are heavily dependent on monthly distributions of surplus food commodities. In some places these are plentiful; in others they don't last the whole four weeks. An Indian family of two in Wyoming had to live for one month on these supplies:

2 pounds of butter
2 pounds of lard
2 pounds of beans
1 pound of dried skim milk
1 sack of corn meal
2 cans of ground beef
2 cans of dehydrated eggs

Even when the commodities are plentiful, the Indians often complain that they do not like the food and that they do not get enough protein. In obtaining food or money from the government, Indians are shown no special favors. A white mother would receive the same ADC help, a disabled white veteran the same pension.

What jobs exist are almost all governmental. To get or keep these few jobs, a person often has to be a "good house Indian" in order to retain the favor of the BIA or the tribal government. Diane Running, at Rosebud, says: "There are three types of Indians—the very poor, the just poor, and those in the tribal office. I know these big shots. They just hire their own relations. No poor Indian gets in. And those men coming from Washington, D.C. They just go to the tribal office. They never come to the back country to talk to us poor Indians. These are all 'one horse' reservations. One big chief telling you what to do. We don't want to have it like this for the rest of our lives."

Both blacks and Indians suffer from discrimination, but again there is a difference. In the white border towns around the reservations, Indians are treated like Negroes in the South, but once Indians get farther away from home, for example to New York or San Francisco, they find themselves the objects of adulation. This, too, is a subtle form of hidden discrimination, even if those who practice it

Schools prided themselves on pictures like these: Indian children arriving at school in blankets and moccasins and, three months later, the same children in collars, jackets and bow ties, dresses and aprons. The object was to make Indians into whites. Often native culture and wisdom were destroyed in the process.

are not aware of it. Again, the Indian is not seen as a real person but as a romantic curiosity.

Nearer the reservations, Indians are still the butts of racist slurs and jokes. The Sioux people of Wanblee, a little town just inside the Pine Ridge reservation, printed this complaint in the local Indian newspaper *The Indian:* "Ever since the white man first occupied our land, we have been the objects of derision and prejudice. The Indian Power sign in the window of the wine cabinet at the Kadoka Municipal Bar is only one of the many subtle insults which are directed towards Indians who live and shop in reservation border towns. The sign has, no doubt, been found quite humorous by many patrons of the bar. We assert that it is insulting and prejudicial. There is a mood sweeping the nation in which minority groups are demanding that they be perceived as people. We concur in this mood and we trust that it will not be long before the white residents of Kadoka shall have advanced to a stage where they, too, can begin to treat their neighbors as people." Kadoka is a white town just outside the reservation.

Indians are suspicious of the way in which the white man's law works. When an Indian who killed a white man was sentenced to death, while a white man who shot and killed an unarmed Indian went unpunished, a Kiowa Indian commented: "Kill a white man, and you die. Kill one of us, and it's different. It's always open season on Indians."

Indians complain of police brutality, as do black people. An Indian civil rights group in Minneapolis has organized its own special patrol. In a car, which is appropriately painted red, they follow police vehicles, watching to see that no Indian's rights are violated. Minneapolis has a fairly large Indian slum. Indians carry one extra burden not shared by other minorities. This is the peculiar status under which they are still treated as wards of the government while on the reservation. Indian law is a jumble of over two thousand different statutes, rules, regulations, and precedents which at every step confound and slow down justice.

A big difference between blacks and Indians lies in their numbers. Twenty million black people can more easily make their voices heard than just 500,000 reservation Indians divided by geography, language, and history. Also, black people are concentrated in large, industrial centers where protests have an immediate impact. Indians are stuck in faraway places from where their voices are only faintly heard. Because of their small numbers, Indians have little voting power outside their own tribes.

All minorities have the same complaint of receiving an inferior brand of segregated education. Indian education is not only inferior, it is a form of warfare against the Indians' identity. It may not have been planned this way, but this is the way it commonly works out.

Before the 1930s the aim to make Indian children "white" was open and outspoken. Indian children were severely punished when they spoke their own language or practiced Indian customs. One special feature of Indian education was, and still is, the tendency to take Indian children away from their parents to distant boarding schools. There is a practical reason for this. Indian homes are scattered over wide regions. It is simpler and more economical to build large boarding schools and concentrate the pupils there than to construct many small neighborhood schools, especially when neighborhood means anything within fifty miles.

But for the Indian children this solution is often a tragedy. A child is taken from his family who loves him and is placed into the care of people who do not speak his language and who know nothing about his way of living. Everything seems cold and strange—the rooms, the food, the behavior expected from him. Boarding school to many

The face of this Sioux youngster at school in South Dakota shows puzzlement. Many school books are not relevant to Indian culture and do not reflect the life this boy knows on the reservation.

Indian children is a prison from where even their own parents cannot rescue them. The shock is so great that many Indian youngsters kill themselves. The school always leaves a scar. Parents feel that their children are neither Indians nor white people, ill-equipped for either world, speaking broken English while having forgotten their own language.

Henry Crow Dog, a Rosebud Sioux, says: "For 8 years, beginning in 1906, I went to the third grade because there was no higher grade when I was a kid. A few times I ran away, but they always caught me and brought me back. Once they threw me in jail for running away." These were the old days.

Modern BIA schools are well-built and look no different from new schools in white suburbs. The teaching is also the same, and that is the trouble. On one reservation, small children were taught from a typical "Dick and Jane" reader. "See father come home from the office. See the children greet him as he puts down his briefcase.

Dad looks into the refrigerator. Dad wants a glass of milk." All this makes little sense to the Indian child, whose father does not go to the office and does not own a briefcase. The Indian child doesn't even know what a refrigerator is. (But he knows how to light a kerosene lamp!)

All education is designed to enable a child to live a normal life in a normal society. But what is normal to the teacher is not normal to her Indian pupils. The teacher's aim is to make the little Indian behave, think, and speak like a white, middle-class child. If the Indian pupil resists this process, if he hangs on to his Indian values, then he is a failure in school. If he is a success at school, he is often a failure at home, a failure as an Indian. Whatever he does he loses. A feeling is instilled in the children that everything Indian is inferior. Even to look like an Indian is bad.

Christine Red Bear says: "I was 13 when I finished the eighth grade. I wanted to go on, but I didn't have the clothes." An Arikara girl remembers: "My folks didn't have money to buy me a coat. When it got cold they gave me a blanket. It was warm and pretty. But I wouldn't go to school wrapped up like that. They would have called me a 'little blanket squaw.' I would have rather frozen to death."

Indians are taught little of their culture and history. When the late Senator Robert Kennedy visited a large Indian school in Idaho, he asked what books they had on Indian history. The library had one book on the subject: *Captive of the Delawares*. It showed an Indian scalping a white child. Indian education has improved greatly in the last ten years, but it still is not improving fast enough.

The Indian has one problem that is shared with no other American— he is a tourist attraction. Many western states advertise themselves as "Indian Land." Many tourists come to "see the Indians." They visit

Indian children like to be taught by Indian teachers who can speak their language and understand their special problems.

the reservations as they would a foreign country. The Indians have mixed feelings about this. A little of the tourists' dollars trickles down to them as they perform in Indian pageants or sell their arts and crafts, but 90 per cent of all the money goes to white shops, white motels, and white restaurants. "We are tired of being exploited for the benefits of others," says a Kiowa dancer, "we should get a bigger cut." "They come up and stick that camera in my face, without asking me, as if I were a tree, or a moose, or something," comments Leonard, a member of the Brulé tribe. "Do they take me for a zoo animal?"

"I am educated. I could make a living elsewhere," says a Pine

Indian children are again being taught by their parents to be proud of their heritage, to take part in Indian ceremonies and dances.

Ridge Indian. "But if I want to stay with my people, I have to put on these phony feathers and pose with my arm around a fat tourist lady. I charge a dollar nowadays. Sometimes I feel like sticking out my tongue when they snap the picture."

"All the concessionaires, the shops that sell Indian art at the national parks, are white," complains Lee Brightman. "They don't allow us Indians to sell our own stuff. That must be changed. And all that junk, 'genuine, authentic Indian beadwork' made in Hongkong or Japan! That should be forbidden."

"What we need above all," says Ruth, a Sioux social worker, "is a new kind of tourist, one who respects us and our right to privacy."

Maybe the greatest difference from other minorities is the Indians' unique culture and history, which often works to keep them divided.

Black Americans often lament the fact that they have been robbed of their cultural heritage. They no longer have a memory of their former tribe, language, or religion. This is sad, but it also gives them unity, a feeling of oneness.

Indians, on the other hand, still speak their own languages, belong to their distinct tribes, retain many of their old customs, and are well informed about their people's history. This means that a man frequently looks upon himself first as a Sioux, a Crow, a Shoshone, or a Cheyenne, and as an Indian only as an afterthought. A Crow is proud of the fact that his grandfather was a trusted scout for Custer. A Cheyenne remembers his grandfather as having counted coup upon that Crow scout. When the two meet, this knowledge will sometimes prevent them from working together as Indians.

Geography plays a part in hindering Indian unity, as tribes are

This photograph shows Indians picketing the movie "A Man Named Horse." Indians no longer accept being depicted as primitive, blood-thirsty savages.

isolated from each other. One tribe has no natural resources, the other derives income from oil leases. One tribe has a small reservation, the other a large. One has a good superintendent, the other a bad. They can't understand each other and must speak English in order to communicate. This makes it harder for them to unite for a common goal, especially when their problems are different. However, a consciousness that they share a common past, a common present, and a common future makes more and more Indians forget old tribal differences.

The Indians' struggle for their civil rights started late, maybe ten years after the beginning of the black liberation movement, but it is gaining momentum now. Indians are not at all like the stereotyped, scowling, deadpan red men of the movies. They like to laugh and have a great sense of humor which often carries a bite. There are therefore smiles mixed in with their anger.

An Indian leader who always does what the white BIA man tells him is often called an Uncle Tomahawk. More recently they call these people Apples,—red on the outside, but white on the inside. The gulf of misunderstanding between whites and Indians is referred to as the Buckskin Curtain. Bumper stickers for cars read: "Custer had it coming!" and "Indians discovered America." A white tourist was handed a button with this description: "Stamp out Colonialism —go away!" And then there are the many new Indian jokes, such as: "What is cultural deprivation? Answer: Being a white, middle-class kid living in a split-level, suburban home watching color TV." Grim, smiling, or both, the struggle for Indian rights is in full swing.

25 ▪ THE TRAIL AHEAD

A voice I will send,
hear me,
the land all over
a voice I am sending,
hear me.
I will live,
I will live.

SWEAT LODGE SONG

We only want the right to live
as other men live.

CHIEF JOSEPH

Tracing the last hundred years of Plains Indian history could make anybody feel sad and depressed. But the 1960s and, especially, the beginning of the 1970s have given the Indians—and their non-Indian friends—new hope. There is a new spirit in the air, a feeling that something great and good is going to happen, and it is Indians who have brought this about by their own efforts.

First, there is a new awareness among whites of what it means to be an Indian today. Never before have Americans been as well informed about Indian culture and history—not all Americans yet, not even most, but a significant number all the same. This new awareness has brought new attitudes, especially among young people. Many whites no longer think that Indians should conform to *their* ways. On the contrary, many young people go to the reservations to learn from the Indians. As one young VISTA worker expressed it: "Indians are beautiful. Why, they were on to democracy and ecology long before us."

Pine Ridge Reservation.

In the last ten years, the Indians found their voice, and this voice was heard throughout the land. It was the voice of the many young, vigorous Indian leaders who emerged during the sixties—Hank Adams, Dennis Banks, John Belindo, Lehman Brightman, Robert Burnette, Vine Deloria, Mel Thom, John Trudell, Tilly Walker and the late Clyde Warrior, to name just a few. Their voices found their way into print. Stan Steiner's book *The New Indians,* published in 1968, was the forerunner of more than a dozen books dealing with Indians, not as historic figures but as energetic participants in the making of a better society. For the first time it was not only a case of white authors writing about Indians for a white audience, but of Indians writing about and for themselves. Among these were authors of great talent and stature, such as Scott Momaday, a Pulitzer Prize winner who wrote *House Made of Dawn* and Vine Deloria, who wrote *Custer Died for Your Sins*.

Indians began to publish newspapers, and the sixties saw the birth of more than a dozen new periodicals written by and for Indians, such as "Akwesasne Notes," "The Warpath," "The Renegade," "The Indian," and many others. Just as numerous were the births of new Indian civil rights organizations, both on and off the reservations. Many of these were started by Indian college students, others by Indians living in city ghettos. A number of the groups were funded by foundations, and members had money to set up workshops and to travel. This made possible many conferences and get-togethers where Indians could discuss common problems. The result was that tribalism was replaced by a sense of Pan-Indianism, a "we are all Indians and brothers" spirit.

Meetings led to common actions. The Indians were "coming out of their cocoons," as one of them described this emergence from their former isolation. Among the first concerted protests was the "fish-in," a demonstration in the state of Washington to help Nisqually Indians in their fight against discriminating fish-and-game laws which made it impossible for the Nisqually to make their accustomed living by catching salmon. White and black sympathizers, as well as Indians, took part in this confrontation.

In 1967, Robert Burnette, one-time president of the Rosebud tribe, led twenty-six Sioux to join the Reverend Dr. Martin Luther King's peace march in New York, in order to draw attention to the Indians' plight. Since then Indian civil rights actions have become more frequent and more spectacular. Indians took part in the Poor Peoples March in Washington, D.C. In 1969, they took over Alcatraz Island in San Francisco Bay, claiming it under sanction of an old treaty made with the Sioux.

Indians also demonstrated against the BIA. A newspaper reported: "Only Indians worked at the Bureau of Indian Affairs facility in Littleton this Thursday. This century-old dream came about for a day when white employees were locked out. Indians, and their white sympathizers, waited for response to their charges that Indian employees have been discriminated against."

From Gallup, New Mexico, to Denver, Colorado, a series of non-violent confrontations took place. The Pine Ridge Sioux occupied Sheep Mountain in the Badlands of South Dakota to demonstrate for a return of the bombing range to their tribe. The range, more than 200,000 acres, was taken over "temporarily" by the air force during World War II.

In the summer of 1970, a group of Indians from Pine Ridge, Rosebud, and Rapid City took over Mount Rushmore and laid claim to the sacred Black Hills. They renamed the monument Crazy Horse Mountain and were soon joined by other Indians from as far away as New York, Minnesota, and California. In all these actions Plains Indians have played an important role.

These peaceful demonstrations have had a number of good results. They not only brought the Indians together, but they also made the older, more timid people and the women take a bold stand. Ruth Hunsinger, a Sioux social worker, says: "At first you couldn't get these old Indian ladies to speak up. Now you can't shut them up! That's progress." It was a lady from Pine Ridge who started the movement to occupy Mount Rushmore. Lizzy Fast Horse is sixty-six years old, but she has scrambled up the steep mountainside—not once, but many times—to bring food and moral support to those camping up there. Indian women have been in the forefront of the fight for Indian rights.

All this has made headlines and given Indians access to the media—TV, radio, national magazines. This, in turn, has had its influence on the mind and conscience of America. The government, too, has been strongly affected. Under President Johnson's War against Poverty program, large funds were made available which brought many improvements to the reservations. Under the Johnson administration an Indian, Robert L. Bennett, was appointed Indian Commissioner, head of the mighty BIA. Louis R. Bruce, another Indian, has been named to the same post by President Nixon.

The policy of termination has been officially abandoned. Some BIA schools have begun experimenting with a new approach to Indian education by building up the Indians' pride in their heritage, stressing their culture, and issuing new textbooks which are relevant to Indian children. Many teachers are now Indians.

Two most significant developments took place on December 2, 1970, in Washington, D.C. Congress and the president gave the sacred Blue Lake, with 48,000 acres, back to the Taos Indians on religious grounds. Up to this date, Indians could sue the government for the value of land that had been taken away from them unlawfully. Usually the compensation, if approved, was based on the price of the land at *the time when it was taken.* During the sixties, an increasing number of tribes received payment this way, but never before had the land itself been given back. Many Plains Indians feel that this sets a precedent. After all, the Black Hills are as sacred to the Sioux and Bear Butte to the Cheyenne as Blue Lake is to the people of Taos.

On the same day Louis R. Bruce, the Commissioner of Indian Affairs, announced far-reaching changes in the set-up of the BIA, "a fundamental reform which puts the future of the nation's Indians into their own hands." They represent, in Mr. Bruce's words, "a fundamental change in philosophy which gives the tribes the right and the authority to take part in the planning and operations of activities that touch their everyday lives."

As President Nixon said in a message to Congress, it is time "to break decisively with the past and to create conditions for a new era in which the Indian future is determined by Indian acts and Indian decisions." Under the new program Indians will be appointed to positions of authority, and the superintendents, who will probably no longer be called by this title which smacks of condescension, will change from being all-powerful dictators to advisers who will help the Indians run the show. Hand in hand with this do-it-yourself program will go a "Buy Indian!" campaign, which is supposed to help Indians take the long road to financial independence.

Earl Old Person, president of the National Congress of American Indians, commented that all this was certainly a step in the right direction. However, together with Mr. Old Person, many Indians feel that it is not yet time to celebrate, that they have heard fine promises before, and that they should adopt a wait-and-see attitude. But all agreed that the new plans sounded good and that the future looks brighter than before.

The Indians who fought so hard for Indian betterment can feel proud that, as *The New York Times* reported, the BIA itself admitted that these "revolutionary reforms have come about in response to long-standing dissatisfaction among the Indians and particularly to the demands of young Indian activists." The fight is not over yet, in fact, it has hardly begun, but Indians now view the future with hope and confidence. Indian Power has won a battle.

"What is Indian Power?" asks a hand-lettered sign in an Indian shop window.

INDIAN POWER means pride in my Indian heritage,
pride in my Indian parents.

INDIAN POWER means a richer, healthier life.

INDIAN POWER means better education
and a meaningful job.

INDIAN POWER means a desire to change from the way
things are now.

INDIAN POWER means holding on to our land.

INDIAN POWER does *not* mean anarchy, it is *not* a communist plot by outside agitators.

INDIAN POWER means LIFE.

The greatest contributions to Indian civil rights, and therefore to the rights of all people, are made by the simple men and women on the reservations who every day make the impossible become a reality. Such a person is Christine Red Bear, a Sioux, who says: "You can't run a person's mind. God gave that mind to a human being as a gift. Because we still have our will power, our own wisdom, our own faith, our own hope—how we should live, what we want to do. We may be poor, but we still have a mind of our own."

The Plains Indians are today a vital part of modern America while stubbornly preserving their own nationhood. Theirs is a proud history and, in a way that nobody planned, it has become part of our history, too. The Red Knights of the Plains with their streaming war bonnets are gone forever, replaced by the Indian teachers, ambulance drivers, cattle raisers, nurses, and social workers of today. But the image of their free life on the Plains, the memory of the prairie's golden age with all its color and pageantry will endure forever, as long as we can savor a starlit night, the rustling of the wind, and the comforting flicker of a campfire.

INDEX